CODEPENDENCY

How to Break Free From the Cycle of
Codependence and Start Taking Care of Yourself

(The Complete Survival Guide for Overcoming
Fear of Rejection)

Daniel Brookins

Published by Oliver Leish

Daniel Brookins

All Rights Reserved

Codependency: How to Break Free From the Cycle of Codependence and Start Taking Care of Yourself (The Complete Survival Guide for Overcoming Fear of Rejection)

ISBN 978-1-77485-120-3

All rights reserved. No part of this guide may be reproduced in any form without permission in writing from the publisher except in the case of brief quotations embodied in critical articles or reviews.

Legal & Disclaimer

The information contained in this book is not designed to replace or take the place of any form of medicine or professional medical advice. The information in this book has been provided for educational and entertainment purposes only.

The information contained in this book has been compiled from sources deemed reliable, and it is accurate to the best of the Author's knowledge; however, the Author cannot guarantee its accuracy and validity and cannot be held liable for any errors or omissions. Changes are periodically made to this book. You must consult your doctor or get professional medical advice before using any of the suggested remedies, techniques, or information in this book.

Upon using the information contained in this book, you agree to hold harmless the Author from and against any damages, costs, and expenses, including any legal fees potentially resulting from the application of any of the information provided by this guide. This disclaimer applies to any damages or injury caused by the use and application, whether directly or indirectly, of any advice or information presented, whether for breach of contract, tort, negligence, personal injury, criminal intent, or under any other cause of action.

You agree to accept all risks of using the information presented inside this book. You need to consult a professional medical practitioner in order to ensure you are both able and healthy enough to participate in this program.

Table of Contents

CHAPTER 1: JUST WHAT DOES CODEPENDENCY MEAN?.... 1

CHAPTER 2: SPOTTING CODEPENDENCE: THE RED FLAGS 26

CHAPTER 3: CO-DEPENDENCY WITH A DRUG ADDICT...... 34

CHAPTER 4: CONQUERING CODEPENDENCY.................... 51

CHAPTER 5: HOW DOES CODEPENDENCY DEVELOP?........ 62

CHAPTER 6: ARE YOU IN A CODEPENDENT RELATIONSHIP? 69

CHAPTER 7: WHEN YOU LOVE TOO MUCH, MAYBE YOU DON'T LOVE 78

CHAPTER 8: CROSSING DE-NILE TO RECOVERY 90

CHAPTER 9: CHANGING A CODEPENDENT RELATIONSHIP 100

CHAPTER 10: HOW TO AVOID CODEPENDENT RELATIONSHIPS 108

CHAPTER 11: WHY CODEPENDENTS HAVE A HARD TIME WITH BREAKUPS 127

CHAPTER 12: CODEPENDENT RELATIONSHIPS 137

CHAPTER 13: THE HABITS OF CODEPENDENT INDIVIDUALS 144

CHAPTER 14: ROAD TO RECOVERY 151

CHAPTER 15: HOW DID YOU GET INTO A CODEPENDENT RELATIONSHIP ANYWAY? 155

CHAPTER 16: FREE YOURSELF FROM CODEPENDENCY AND TAKE CONTROL OF YOUR LIFE 159

CHAPTER 17: HOW TO FIX CODEPENDENT RELATIONSHIPS 174

CONCLUSION 192

Chapter 1: Just What Does Codependency Mean?

When you think about being independent, what comes to your mind? Does it mean that you own a vehicle, are an independent homeowner, and strive for what you want all on your own? Does it mean to love yourself in every way or take care of yourself? Is it you know what you believe in, and you aren't afraid to stand up for your truth? Maybe it's all the above. The fact is that everyone is independent, and we all show it in different ways and define it differently. According to the definition given by Webster's dictionary, independent means we don't let others control us, as one is dependent solely on themselves. According to the Oxford dictionary, an individual is both capable of thinking or acting for oneself and will not allow others to influence them.

Now, take a moment to think about what **codependent** is. Does it mean the opposite of the above definitions? Does it mean that you obtain lifts from others, rent from landlords, or are not thoroughly ambitious without the help of others? Does codependency mean that you can't love yourself without knowing or being reassured by trusted people around you? Is it you aren't sure what you believe in yet because you rely on someone else's opinions? Codependence may be the opposite of independence. However, because of the world and society we grew up in, codependence seems like a 'bad' word. We think and say that if someone is codependent, they are controlling or dysfunctional. Is this true, though? Is it okay to be codependent and independent at the same time? Is it even possible? There are many definitions offered by various dictionaries, among others, for independence. However, all sources provide the same meaning for codependency. They state that **codependence is an emotional or**

psychological reliance aside from oneself that requires constant support accompanied by neediness and other personality traits.

When you think carefully about the meaning of codependency, everyone shares some qualities of a codependent person. We are all needy in our way. We all ask for the support of our family and friends. Everyone relies on and depends on others to make them happy in one form or another. When the ones closest to us don't meet our needs, it can lead to disappointments. Disappointments happen when we expect things from our friends, families, and partners. All the accepted definitions of codependence state it is a disorder of some form or another. However, we must understand that codependence only becomes a problem if someone is reliant on someone else for all aspects of their lives. It is as if someone cannot think for themselves thoroughly or trust themselves sufficiently, so they rely and depend on others to support them. In this chapter, we will understand what codependency is so we can make informed judgements regarding the term.

Codependency is more than being needy or controlling; it's where an individual has an overwhelming amount of low self-esteem that controls their behaviour. We must first understand the intentions behind a person's actions before assuming that they are desperate, or as Webster states, psychologically inclined to rely on the support from others. An individual may seem like a lonely, depressed, impulsive, perfectionist on the outside, but what is truly going on inside the person's mind? Many people in codependent relationships may make excuses for their partner or develop an unstable partnership. There is no set medical definition for this psychological illness. However, some symptoms and personality traits are:

- Low self-esteem.
- Low confidence.
- Perfectionism.
- Reduced sense of values and morals.

- Misunderstood perspective of boundaries.
- People-pleasing tendencies.
- Difficulty communicating and interacting with others.
- Dependency.
- Struggles with internal control that appears controlling towards others and situations.
- Addictive personality.
- Excessive neediness.

So, what does this all mean? Is codependency a psychological disorder? Can it be treated? Does it just affect the individual, or does it involve other people? I am sure you have heard the term monkey see monkey do. This phrase means that what the younger generation sees from their peers and older loved ones, they may follow as they grow older. Someone who is excessively dependent on others may have learnt the behaviour from their peers when they were young. Usually brought up within a dysfunctional family, they will see their future relationships as addictive, which can significantly affect their perspective of a healthy relationship. A codependent individual often becomes involved or stays in a relationship that is mentally, physically, emotionally, and intimately abusive. It can affect everyone in the family and other associations such as friends, co-workers, and employers.

So, where does a codependent personality stem from? Many individuals grow up within a dysfunctional family with underlying complications such as addiction, abuse, or physical and mental illness. These complications can create negative feelings of anxiety, anguish, resentment, disgrace, rejection, or denial. The main reason dysfunctional families stay dysfunctional (leading to unstable and imbalanced intimate relationships), is that they don't deal with their struggles. Because of the denial they feel, they can never own up to their true sentiments, which decreases the self-awareness needed to build healthy partnerships. These families stay in a bubble by detaching themselves from their deeper feelings of disgust. As a result, avoiding feelings and problems makes it difficult for them to trust anyone else due to an unhealthy distrust for themselves.

Children have people they look up to throughout their lives; when they witness rejection and avoidance, they may make the same mistakes and develop the same behaviours as their role models. Over an extended period, the individual develops a low sense of self-esteem. This promotes actions of putting others above themselves, as the need for approval and gratitude becomes their primary focus. If someone outside the family can teach the children positive behaviours, they will have a fighting chance to follow their path. However, in most cases, children will follow their parents because they are their primary role models. A codependent will deny their feelings by changing the subject or controlling a problem to suit the needs of others over themselves. When someone shows signs of low self-esteem, there is a higher chance that this individual will put the needs of others above their own. This is because the need for approval and gratitude becomes the primary focus of a codependent's needs. If they cannot find someone to please or go above and beyond for, they will hide behind their work or feed their harmful cravings with bad habits such as nail-biting and obsessive organising. Sometimes, it can even lead to alcoholism and drug addiction or gambling and excessive sexual behaviour.

Aside from the best intentions behind their actions, they can develop unhealthy patterns of behaviour. These patterns may include the individual justifying her husband's abusive ways, or the father manipulating a situation to excuse their child's behaviour. The more these behaviours continue to happen, the longer the person stays dependent on their unhealthy relationships. With the excessive reliance on and the enablement from the partner, they trigger a reward system inside the brain because it has been wired to feel satisfied when the individual feels needed. The codependent then sees themselves as being the victim in almost every relationship, so they feel extreme empathy when they see the same weakness in others. In the next chapter, we will look deeper into the characteristics of a codependent person and explain what makes them tick and why. For now, what follows is a list of traits a codependent individual cannot escape.

• They mistake the feeling of love for pity. Since they take pity on others, they feel that 'rescuing' them comes from a place of love—not being dependent.

• Oversensitivity to a lack of personal recognition. The person becomes deeply hurt when someone does not notice their efforts.

• They have a problem with letting go of an unhealthy relationship because of abandonment issues.

• An excessive need for attention and approval.

• The need to control everything without the ability to be self-aware.

• They cannot define their feelings or control them.

- An overwhelming fear of being alone, neglected, or abandoned.
- Fear of honesty; they do not want to hurt others or themselves.
- Pent up anger and frustration.
- Problems with making decisions (big or small).
- Struggles with communication and interaction.

The good news is that people can break the destructive cycle of codependency with motivation and the desire for change. The first step is to educate yourself and realise the cycle of addiction and abuse. It is vital to have the willingness to change and understand what codependency means; otherwise, you could fall into a toxic relationship and continue to self-sabotage one's life. One of the unhealthiest relationships that many codependents fall into are related to narcissism.

Narcissism or Codependency?

Much like a narcissist, a dependent person will turn the focus onto themselves to have reassurance and spotlight control. It's not that they cannot handle being in the outer circle; it's that they need constant reassurance and attention to help with their insecurities. Unlike a narcissist, a codependent doesn't know they are doing it and often cannot control themselves when they do. Now that we have touched on narcissism, what exactly is narcissism?

Narcissistic personality disorder is where someone is self-centred and thrives on the failures of others to get ahead. We will touch more on narcissism in chapter three, but for now, we need to understand the differences between the narcissist and the codependent. There is one key difference between narcissism and codependency. A codependent is entirely selfless, and it manifests itself by the need to be in control, neediness, and perfectionism. A narcissist represents self-centeredness and shows it through grandiose superiority, a charming nature, and a lack of empathy for others. Narcissists and codependents have similar thought patterns and needs; however, they each show them and behave differently to these thoughts and needs. They struggle with defining who they are, have insecurities, and fear what others think of them.

People who have narcissistic personality disorder focus on themselves and desire excessive attention while showing no empathy for others. They are charming only to exploit the needs of their victims to get what they want, one of their many manipulative tactics. They rely on others to give them what they want rather than going out to get what they desire themselves. Most of all, they continually look for the 'narcissistic supply' by using the **idealise, devalue, and discard approach** upon their victims (more about this in chapter three).

Codependents do things a little differently because they always concern themselves with others and how they feel, as born people-pleasers. They feel the need to control others and situations because they think this approach is what's best for the third party. One of the codependent's traits is that they have too much empathy for others, so they then disregard themselves. They thrive on the feeling of being needed and will do everything in their power to perfect something, control someone, or push limits if it means that they get the approval of their target.

As you can see, it is effortless for the codependent to be the victim of a narcissist. And, for the narcissist, it is easy to become the codependent's target. As the codependent tries hard to please the narcissist, the narcissist continuously receives his narcissistic supply. Abuse appears in the devalue stage, in which the codependent becomes used to and tries to rescue or fix the narcissist without realising the narcissist cannot change.

Are You Suffering a Dysfunctional Relationship?

With the information you have read so far, can you be sure you know someone displaying codependent traits? Do you feel as though you might exhibit some or all of the above characteristics yourself? Whichever it is and no matter which end of the spectrum you are on, it is always useful to know when and if you are in a dysfunctional relationship. An unhealthy relationship relates to abusive traits where one person is not entirely truthful, or they feel the need to control and manipulate everything. In a dysfunctional relationship, communication can often become misinterpreted, which sets you up for unnecessary abusive relationship patterns. The problem is that neither person feels as if they are doing or saying anything wrong because each individual has their way of expressing themselves. It's natural to have arguments and disagreements in every relationship we are in, as no friendship or partnership is perfect. A relationship becomes unstable when unhealthy discussions happen all the time. Sadly, neither party wants to end the relationship because they feel a secure attachment or familiarity where the lives of both revolve solely around each other. For example, a narcissist will charm their victim and sprinkle a little glimpse of hope that things will change. Then, they will revert to their manipulative and controlling ways. A codependent will justify their partner's behaviour by sacrificing their own needs and convincing themselves they 'love' this person.

What is a Healthy Relationship?

A healthy relationship is where the positive aspects of a relationship outweigh the negative, and when there is an equal amount of effort going into it on both sides. It's where you can lift someone in their darkest moments and love them unconditionally through the good and the bad. A relationship becomes dysfunctional when negativity and heartache become the norm, and the strength of the bond weakens. Eventually, you may feel as though you are living with a partner who now seems like a roommate. It takes skill to compromise and resolve conflict in any connection you have as that involves effective communication, and not everyone is an expert in this field. If you feel you might be in a relationship where you feel trapped, resent your partner or friend, or cannot seem to agree on anything anymore, you are probably in a dysfunctional relationship.

When someone is in a dysfunctional relationship, they might feel as though there is no way out and no way to overcome the endless arguments and restless nights. However, most couples struggle with understanding why they are even fighting. Unhealthy relationships follow these same patterns. It's vital to recognise unhealthy relationships for what they are before the partners can work on it thoroughly as a team.

The Blame Game

It's good to look into a relationship and see if either partner appears to be the victim in every scenario, and if the other comes up with various excuses about arguments not being their fault. If one partner always has to defend themselves and their actions while attacking the other, a **blame game** is likely to be happening in the relationship. Whether you notice yourself doing it, these actions and beliefs are part of blaming the other party and vice versa. Using blame as a weapon is a hurtful technique, as it can sometimes cloud our vision in seeing what's truly going on. It forces the victim of blame to second guess everything to the point of self-destruction, and it's because they want to believe their partner or friend has their best interests at heart. The reason someone would blame you for something is actually that they are projecting their faults and mistakes onto you.

Instead of blaming someone for something you think they have done, approach them with questions and take responsibility for your actions. If you blame them for something, they will blame you, and your communication and bond will fall apart. Find out why they may point blame because often it stems from underlying insecurity. For example, if they are accusing you of cheating, ask yourself why they would assume this. Have you cheated? Are they cheating? Is there a jealousy trait that is taking over? Does it come down to power and control? In this example, if your partner is difficult to talk to, try to write what you need to say, reread it, then bring the conversation to the table to resolve the problem. This will diffuse the argument rather than fuel it.

Constant Threats Against Known Weaknesses

As you get to know one another, you find out each other's weaknesses and personal fears. One commonly found behaviour pattern in unhealthy relationships is that one partner exploits their loved one's vulnerabilities by giving them ultimatums. For example, if you are in a heated argument and your partner has a vehicle, they might say 'I'm leaving until you can calm down.' The intention behind this voiced opinion is that they expect you to apologise, or else they will leave because they know one of your fears is abandonment. You might tell your loved one that you will go if they cannot learn how to get along with you. This control is something a codependent may use against you because they do not know how to express themselves better.

The threat to leave can be misconstrued if the action is not complete; the relationship will end. The only time you should ever threaten to leave a relationship is if you intend on breaking off the link permanently. Otherwise, if used just to hurt each other, distrust and conflict will continue to build in the relationship, which fixes nothing. You never know when one day, the threat of leaving could be the tip of the iceberg and a breakup you didn't want follows. Voice your opinion in different ways by saying what you mean and doing what you say.

Controlled vs Control

Every relationship, whether friend, co-worker or significant other, goes through the **power stage** of a relationship. This stage comes after the **honeymoon stage** and is usually when both parties know each other on a deeper level. The **control stage** in a relationship is when partners test the boundaries and breaking points of the relationship. It allows both parties to figure out who is the **'alpha'** or **'beta'** with giving and taking control. Treating people like this is a horrible way of looking at things. No one should ever be alpha or beta in any relationship, as both should put in the same amount of effort and commitment into the relationship. If this attitude continues, one person may become submissive as an attempt to stop the war between you both, while the other becomes dominant and displays how significant they think they are.

Throughout a relationship with a controlling person, the other partner will justify the controlling partner's actions, allowing the latter to continue the control. In a healthy relationship, both individuals come together as a team and sort out any differences and perspectives to come up with positive solutions. No one makes important decisions without the consent of the other; therefore, no one feels inferior. By looking at the relationship in this way, it creates stronger bonds and longer-lasting partnerships.

Holding Grudges

This form of abuse is a more silent weapon, only used in the matter of conflict. It brings up events from the past in the form of a new argument. Therefore, partners never forget old arguments, even after solving them. The best way to overcome grudges is to build trust, genuinely forgive all parties, and let go of the past. People who harbour grudges usually have underlying insecurities within themselves. When animosity or a past conflict comes out, the partners play it as a weapon to hurt, manipulate, and control their significant other. These people often feel victimised, mistreated, or resent previous solutions because they think they didn't win.

Violation in Boundaries

People hold **boundaries** dear to their hearts, much like values. We can set these limits in place to allow us to succeed and protect ourselves. When we love someone (or think we do), we often allow them to cross these boundaries because we convince ourselves it won't happen again. However, the other party knows this and will continue to push your limits to see how far they can go. Sometimes, the party such as a codependent may not realise they are pushing boundaries because, in their best attempts to please you, they are going behind your back, breaking trust and not offering their reasons for trying to push those boundaries.

This attitude is childish—all children will push limits and their parents' boundaries to get away with things and learn from that. A healthy relationship does not test the waters because of the respect the partners have for themselves and others. Just like unhealthiest patterns in any relationship, each way of doing things will stem from an ulterior motive or problems within oneself. Pushing boundaries results from someone with deep feelings of what is yours is mine, and there should be nothing hidden between us. This may be true, but it doesn't mean that you must go looking for trouble, or the 'truth' without first talking to your partner. Violation of privacy and boundaries comes from a deep distrust and disrespect for one another. Once there is no more trust, nothing can hold you two together.

All relationships should be full of respect, love, commitment, trust, and loyalty. It takes a great deal of work to have a healthy, intimate relationship. This is also true for important family and social connections in one's life. For example, if you don't try to contact your parents and vice versa, how can you expect to hold a solid foundation for a closer bond? To have a healthy relationship, you must also be in a healthy mental and physical state. Someone with codependent traits can think they are doing their best when, in reality, they have never seen a healthy relationship and have always followed their role models (who would also be codependent). They may not have learnt effective ways to communicate or love themselves deeply; therefore, they will act abusively and won't understand until a relationship has failed. However, using this as an excuse will make you seem more at fault than you intend to show. In the second section of this book, you will learn how to break out of this cycle and develop closer bonds for longer-lasting relationships.

Chapter Summary

Codependency is challenging to understand and is not recognised as a mental disorder. The main dictionary definitions state that codependency involves an individual who is psychologically inclined to rely on and depend on others. From a theoretical standpoint, we need not define codependency as a mental illness because we are all codependent. Narcissistic personality disorder is when the person believes the world will fall into their hands no matter the consequences; the same goes for codependency. The percentage of individuals falling into unhealthy patterns and dysfunctional relationships is steadily increasing. Therefore, it's paramount to understand the nature of healthy relationships, understand respect, and create healthy boundaries and habits before trying to share the universe with

someone else. In this chapter, you learnt about:
- What Codependency means.
- About the nature of dysfunctional relationships.
- Where the behavioural traits of codependency stem from.
- The link between narcissism and codependency.
-

In the next chapter, you will discover the critical red flags that you should look out of within dysfunctional relationships, as well as different forms of dysfunctional relationships.

Chapter 2: Spotting Codependence: The Red Flags

Though it's easy to read about codependency on paper, many people in codependent relationships have a hard time actually identifying it and seeing how it affects them in real life. Therefore, it's important that you become aware of the "red flags"; by knowing the signs that codependency has reared its head in your relationship.

The most common signs of codependence include the following:

-You allow and encourage each other's bad behavior.

Enabling each other's bad behavior includes making excuses for addictions and bad behavior. It can also involve blaming yourself for your partner's faults.

-Your needs and preferences are minimized.

Being in a codependent relationship involves one party having to put aside his or her own feelings, needs and wants in order to accommodate their partner.

-You become the worst version of yourself. Bad behaviors and habits become part your life, so know that being in a codependent relationship won't allow you to improve. Most of the time, people in a codependent relationship find themselves simply becoming the worst version of themselves rather than the best.

-You feel bad about yourself, and the type of person you are now.

Codependent people know deep down that what they're doing isn't good for them, and is generally detrimental to their wellbeing. However, codependency can become similar to any addiction in that it is a hard cycle to break. Hence, those in a codependent relationship tend to develop a negative sense of self.

-You need validation and acceptance to feel good.

Codependency reduces people's self-worth. In other words, codependent people tend to judge their own worth mostly by how other people perceive them. Therefore, it isn't uncommon for codependent people to look for validation in order to feel good about themselves and to perceive themselves in a positive sense.

-You find it hard to communicate with your partner.

The tendency will be to put your own needs aside, and to accommodate your partner at all costs. Therefore, codependent people find a hard time genuinely communicating with their partners about what they want, what they feel, and what they need.

-You become obsessive about your relationship.

Your relationship takes the center stage, and has become the top priority in your life to an unhealthy extent. You invest all of your time in trying to please your partner and have nothing else to fall back on when you fail. The problem with this is that you end up defining yourself by how well your relationship is going. If it doesn't go well, you end up having great difficulty coping and dealing with these problems.

- You are anxious to please.

The need to please your partner also takes up most, if not all, of your time. Therefore, you find yourself constantly anxious in trying to meet their needs and wants, even though it goes against what you believe in or what you want to do. You may also experience feelings of fear and anxiety when expressing something that contradicts your partner.

- You continually second-guess yourself.

Codependency greatly affects self-esteem, and causes great amounts of self-doubt. Therefore, codependent people find themselves always second-guessing themselves, stemming from the fear that others may not agree with what they say or do. They also become debilitated by the risk that people may judge them negatively or perceive them in a bad light.

- You feel inadequate.

This is highly related to the previous point. Codependents can become so doubtful of themselves and what they can do and can often become haunted by a sense of incompetence or inadequacy.

- You have difficulties with boundaries.

There is a general difficulty encountered when having to say no, and setting up boundaries can be particularly challenging for codependent people. This boundary issue can also apply when trying to separate ones own identity from that of your partner.

- You distance yourself from your loved ones.

Isolating yourself from loved ones is a common symptom of codependency. Given the earlier point that the codependent relationship becomes the main priority, there may also be the fear of having loved ones disapprove of the relationship's dynamic, and how it is playing out.

- You lose your sense of identity.

Codependent relationships entail that you give over most of your time and your resources to address your partner's needs. In doing so, you find yourself losing your own identity, and having difficulty determining who you are when your partner isn't around.

-You become sort of an "emotional sponge".

Codependent individuals tend to absorb or soak up the negative criticism that is directed at them, and often allow these negative feelings to build up to an impossible point. This can cause a lot of other related problems, like depression, anxiety, and generally compromised health.

-You find yourself being passive about the things that happen to you.

Codependents may become so used to catering to others that they become passive about the negative things that happen to them. This passive behavior can become particularly harmful when you become the victim of abuse.

-You find that the other aspects of your life are falling into detriment.

Though relationships are technically only one aspect of life, codependent people can find that the destructive effects of their relationship seeps into other parts of their daily living. For example, codependent people often run the risk of becoming depressed. If this does happen, they may overlook taking care of their health, performing well at work, and the like.

-You feel lonely.

Though codependent people are in a relationship, they may still feel lonely. Remember that should you be in a codependent relationship, you may not actually be recognized as your own person. Your voice may be drowned out by your partners' and your own personality may not be allowed to shine through.

-You find yourself relying on someone else completely.

Codependent people also often find themselves completely reliant on their partners for resources and care. Though expecting our partners to care for us is completely normal, over-reliance is often the case when referring to codependent relationships.

-You find difficulty when asking for help, no matter how necessary.

Keeping what you feel to yourself is part of why codependence is a vicious cycle.

Everyone needs help sometimes, but codependence can make this difficult to see, particularly since a codependent relationship greatly affects your sense of self-worth. Therefore, many individuals stuck in a codependent relationship often hide their realities from other people. Many are also trapped in denial, and may immediately fall back on making excuses for their reality.

Aside from these red flags, it's also important to remember that codependency was first recognized in terms of alcoholism; therefore, you need to recognize the occurrence of codependence in relation to addiction. If you or your partner have an addiction (drugs, alcohol, etc.), it is also likely that you're in a codependent relationship that enables addictive or destructive behavior.

Chapter 3: Co-Dependency With A Drug Addict

Another basic addiction for a co-dependent is substance addiction. The severity of the addiction increases with the seriousness of the drug. Exemplifying, many of the adolescents or general public get into drugs through their peers or partners, via marijuana. Now as the debate is held strong, marijuana is also regarded as a gateway drug where the subject after contact with pot becomes quite aware about most of the drugs in the market as well as accessibility of the same. Now, with emotional turmoil, the subjects get involved in climbing the drugs ladder higher and higher, only to destroy themselves forever. As debated marijuana may or may not have the addictive abilities, but if you wake up and roll a joint to surprise your partner every morning as well as roll one after another a dozen joints per day to keep your lover addict happy, then you are indeed loosening your own turmoil resorting to pot. If in his/her absence too, pot has proved out to be a necessity to calm yourself down, then you are successfully an addicted co-dependent on pot.

When drug intensity increases to Acid, X-tablets, Coke and 'etch', the addiction takes a strong toll that advocates almost a sense of spiritual communication and wavelength match of the subject with the addict, due to the drugged effect of the former. This feeling turns into a paranoia and addiction that disproves the presence or absence of the addict-lover to be drugged.

Another aspect of the co-dependent assisting or supporting their partners is through doing the extra work; earn the extra money to meet the extra-ends. This can result in undue financial obligation of the drug addict toward the subject, which further steers the process to addiction and passive addiction being high. The subject involves in entertaining and finding comfort in the aura of the drug-addict and the daily lines of white Goddess, to finally end up finding power and relief through drugs by believing in the sanctity of the deed as love.

Either ways, it's the co-dependent who does not go into rehab or counselling after the loved one is treated for the addiction. Follow the end of the book to find a brief guide to take control of yourself from being an addict and help your loved one get ashore as well!

Love and Marriage as Co-dependency Parameter #2

Both love and marriage are interexchange able parameters of commitment with a partner through co-existence. When the format of the relationship takes course of longer time, co-dependency can start as part of the love addiction.

Love as Co-dependency Parameter

A love-addict is a precise character that has issues similar as co-dependency that are crucial and serious in battling addictions. A love addict refuses to find interest in anything but to love everything with a quench that a co-dependent also thirsts to, but both of them vehemently try to mask the abandonment and loneliness inside.

Addictions of Fantasy Story Tales: love addicts have an idea of their love affairs to be similar to fairy-tale kind of stories, formats, settings and fantasies. They dream about their prince charming, see their Cinderella on every road, nook and cranny and are delusional when a relationship starts. This can result in bad companionship skills instilling a dysfunction in the practical aspect of expectations about the partner.

Challenges: another aspect of a Love-centred co=dependency is the constant sense of wanting to hurdle various challenges and hurdles that might equate to getting disinterested in people within a short period.

Fear of abandonment: another prevalent similarity of co-dependency and love addiction is the constant fear of abandonment. This fear is registered from a sense of abandonment or loss that persists all through the relationship.

Undue time on relationships and aspects of co-existence

Avoidance addicts from Love addicts: avoidance addicts are usually focussed on the aspects of alcohol, drugs, sexual appetite and work rather than romance and other aspects. This is the first signal of the person being a love addict who wants to rush things in the fear of their co-dependence. We all feel like having a strong evidence of our ideologies, motives and desires, but a love addict is attracted to people who tend to avoid situation of frankness and who display certain shyness or discomfort towards the aforementioned topics.

Relief by fantasising about more than one Love becoming a burden or reason to be confined to a certain sense of disappointment, distress and agony.

Marriage as Co-dependency Parameter

The oldest conventions and traditions of marriage holds it as a sacred communion of body, mind and soul of a person under God's will and public blessing. Marriage was emphasised to be arranged by the parents, independent of the groom and bride's wish. This ancient practise proposed marriages as a strict parameter of co-dependency.

Marriage is practised by many societies as the sole communion and embodiment of co-dependence. As ancient-er it gets, scriptures dictate what a woman's responsibility is towards her husband in keeping the health of co-dependent relationship of marriage. These movements aimed at co-dependency in marriages often bring about a sense of duty of adjusting, compromising and adapting to the partner's requests.

The habituation of co-existence is largely experienced in the institution of marriage through self-destructive and sabotaging aspects of co-dependency. It is not every marriage, but some of the wedded bliss that accounts to turn into a co-dependent relationship.

Biblical aspects of co-dependency are relied on the oldest aspects maintaining a relationship of a couple intact with either becoming the enabler and the other, an abuser. It relies in healthy co-existence through compromise, adjustments and blind-faith on god's rules and ways about matrimony.

In the course of a long marriage, both the partners become annoyed and irritated with each other or so and start to resent each other's company and try to resolve by becoming co-dependent through anger, withdrawal, overly caretaking, domineering, responsibility, spying, doubt and regret.

Parenthood and Family as Co-dependency Parameter #3

Often times all the above leads to dysfunction in marriages, this becomes the cause and effect of troubled parenthood and dysfunction in Family, on a whole. The troublesome marriages end up in a divorce or separation, for which the children bears the fruits.

Parenthood as a Co-dependency Parameter

Co-dependent Parents

Co-dependency of Fear in Parenthood is one of the most general occurrence of co-dependency in parenthood.

Over consciousness: one of the effective stabilising of a parent's co-dependency is through their acts from over-consciousness. As they are perpetually worried about their kids, they establish a argument that is paranoid, whenever the kid raises a topic.

Holding authority over all personal decisions: is one category of parents, who tend to believe that they have the right to exert authority over all of their child's decisions, regardless of their importance.

Over-bonding Parenthood: some parents try to bond too much to their kids by becoming the creepy or interfering element in their personal space, peace and calmth that the kid grows up to be paranoid of everything in their life. For example, a kid hates anyone touching their stuff in a shared hotel room. This owes to the fact that her mom had a nosy habit of going through her personal belongings by utilising the excuse of cleaning her room. One day in her hostel, the friends, unaware of this fact, try to surprise her by cleaning the room. She reacts vehemently to their surprise. This is one of the impacts of over-bonding parents who create an image of creepiness or endless interference on their account, toward the kids.

Having No respect for the Kids: another category of poorly co-dependent parenthood is reflected through having no respect for the kids. This arises from a constant judgement of the kid being irresponsible, incompetent, unable and worthless, from the parent. Hence, the parent consistently makes remarks that emphasises their lack of respect, honour and positivity towards the kid. This recurrent disapproval from the parent can mould the kid into a terribly depressed, clueless, dishonest and useless person with perpetual failures.

Comparing the kids with others: this is one of the worst aspects of poor parenthood, where the parents keep on comparing their kid's and expectation against the peer group of neighbour's, brother's, sister's, relative's kids grades, achievements and scores.

Biased relationship with kids: sometimes parents end up treating kids separately within the family. Exemplifying, in a family of kids- 1 boy and 1 girl, mother's undue affection towards the son, can instil a sense of abandonment for the girl child while a father's attachment towards the daughter can result in the son in the family feeling detached from the dad.

Control-freaks: yes, this category of co-dependent parents also exist. Parents who exert and execute their desires upon the dreams and ambitions of the kids figure into this category of control-freaks. They specify hard and fast rules that control the academic and personal life of their kids, without any relations, breaks or rewards for the same.

Recurrent punishments: another aspect of co-dependent parenthood is where the parents involve the kids in recurrent and regular punishments for their deeds. Control-freaks type of parents establishes hard rules, for which they make strict punishments, regardless of the deed. This instils a sense of fear, hatred and discontent towards the parents.

Unsatisfied attitude: this arises from the perpetual comparisons and discontent from the parents towards their kids. Gradually the child ends up disbelieving in his or her abilities, skills, talents and dreams owing to the feeling of not making the parents ever happy. Lack of appreciation for good deeds, mature decisions and responsibilities bring about a constant depression and despair in the kid.

Perfectionists: some parents become too inflexible that they deny any fun or frolic to their kids. Their ideals of perfection remain the limits, restrictions and discontent for the kids. This inflexibility not only damages the parent-child relationship, but also brings about mentally unsatisfied kids.

Co-dependent Kids

Co-dependent kids are the kind of children who believe that their parents should be responsible for each of their deeds. Hence, they consult and counsel with their parents to achieve anything or take any a decision. This is due to their psychological belief of lacking confidence in the self about taking any decision by themselves. Co-dependent kids fear of the day that their parents will not be there, to guide them. Some of the main cause and effects of co-dependent behaviour towards parents are:

1) Worried Attitude: the first and foremost cause and effect of a co-dependent child is his worried attitude. The worried behaviour is consistent regarding taking any a decision, doing anything or even forming an opinion about something.

2) Perpetually Clueless: almost all co-dependent kids share this attitude as they feel clueless when they lack guidance from their parents. They do not know of an independent route or path unless guided by their parents beforehand.

3) Empathise with parents too much: co-dependent kids empathise with their parents too much that their experiences

are all lived by through their parent's shoes. Empathy involves relaxing one's own desires that the subject ends up feeling more than obliged to the parents.

4) Call parents for everything: a co-dependent child ends up seeking his parents counsel under all circumstances, regardless of its importance. There is no independent identity, plan or resolutions and hence the child lacks any motive of the own, to achieve anything.

5) Worried about crowd or loneliness: another primary defining aspect of a co-dependent child is his or her worry about facing the crowd or being lonely, in the absence of parents. Co-dependent kids cannot are highly introverted sans their parents support.

6) Love Addict: another important category of co-dependent children are the love-addicts, Casanovas or playboys. This kind of children become addicted to hunting for love due to the detachment they feel with their parents. Co-dependent children who miss their parents love, care and affection believes in being content

through a relationship or constant dosage of intimacy shared with a person.

7) Having parent's dream as own dream and none of the own: often, the kids who are overly co-dependent, end up believing in their own existence as something that is heavily obliged to making their parent's dreams come true.

8) Self-sabotage: when a child ends up believing that parent's dreams, fantasies and desires are above their own, they end up sabotaging their own commitments, desires, fancies and whims to pave way for the parents dreams and ambitions coming true.

9) No self-respect: a co-dependent kid has very low self-confidence, self-esteem and self-respect that he does not believe in his own potential of realising his dreams, as there are none. Gradually such a kid turns into a terrible automaton without no individual aim, personal success or ambition.

Family as a Co-dependency Parameter

Co-dependent parenthood and co-dependent parent-child relationship in the longer run can induce a dysfunction in the entire family. Certain times the co-dependency manhandled in a marriage are a cause of dysfunction in the family. A co-dependence scenario of troubling parenthood gives rise to co-dependent kids who pave way for a dysfunction in the family, on a full scale.

Some of the harmful effects of dysfunction in a family due to co-dependence is through

1) Lack of emotional contentment is one of the basic effects of a dysfunctional family as the kids and the parents both feel that the family is draining much of their positivity into it, rather than making themselves feel positive or content.

2) Lack of Communication instils a huge gap in the family members as in the due course of time, each family member resorts to avoiding the company of the rest for one's own peace.

3) Divorce: this is one of the direct effects of poorly handled marital co-dependencies. When co-dependency becomes irresolvable, parents can end up

in suggesting divorce or separation, which can directly affect the physical, mental and emotional psyche of the kid.

4) De-valuing the suggestion of the family members: with the growing discomfort, individual members of the family ends up valuing the suggestions and remarks of other family members on a lesser and increasingly lesser honour.

5) Lack of Love: another important effect upon a family owing to inter-dependent co-dependent parameters is the experience of immense lack of love. This instils a feeling of needing to search for love outside the family, even becoming a love addict in the process.

6) Lack of Self-respect: another quite important aspect of co-dependency in a family is the lack of self-respect among individuals as well as lack of respect for each other. This induces a feeling of constantly minimising the value of one's family as well as dismissing the same with worthlessness. This also instils in the family, a sense of lack of aims, ambitions and achievements.

7) Lack of Freedom individually, due to controlling, hard and punishing authoritarian patriarchy by the co-dependent parents/ kids;

Chapter 4: Conquering Codependency

Codependency may lead to different long term problems such as depression, low self-esteem, health problems, career problems and relationship difficulties. Co-dependents often feel trapped, abused and they often feel that they are unable to trust anyone.

But there is hope. If you are a codependent, it is not too late. You can either end a codependent relationship or shape it to become more healthy and balanced. You can still reclaim your life and take control.

Here are the steps on how you could conquer and cure codependency:

Acknowledge that there is a problem – Codependents are constantly in denial. They routinely deny that they have a problem. The first step in conquering codependency is to acknowledge it. You have to accept the fact that there is a problem. Be realistic. Realize that the relationships that you are in are not balanced. You have to recognize that the people you care about are taking advantage of you- your friends, family, spouse, kids, siblings or parents. Once you acknowledge and accept this, then you are on your way to recovery.

Make a decision to do whatever it takes to conquer codependency – You have to make a tough decision to wage a war against codependency. After you have acknowledged that codependency is your problem, this is the time to decide to take steps that are necessary to end your codependency and make your life better. This is very difficult to do, but once you have made up your mind and you made the commitment to make positive changes in your life, there is no turning back. Everything will eventually become easier, lighter and you will be genuinely happy and feel more fulfilled.

Get some help – It is necessary to talk to someone you trust about your codependency and the steps that you will take to end it. You can talk to an emotionally healthy family member or friend or you could see a mental health professional. You can also seek the help of spiritual leader that you respect and you can trust. The support of the people around you will push you into the direction of recovery.

Focus on yourself – This is very important. If you want to conquer codependency, you have to focus on your own needs, wants and dreams. Take time to ask yourself – what do I really want? If you find yourself answering based on what your partner wants, ask yourself again and again until you get the real answer. If you are a codependent, you have spent so much time and effort focusing on other people's wants and needs that you have already forgotten your own desires and needs. Now is the time to be in touch with your own needs and your own desire. Do you want to go back to school or start your own business or maybe travel around the world? Acknowledge your needs, feelings, emotions and your dreams.

Practice Self-Love — Self-love is not the same with narcissism. In fact, narcissistic people may appear confident on the outside, but deep inside, they despise themselves and feel inadequate. People who love themselves, on the other hand, accept themselves unconditionally. They do not take abuse and disrespect. They do not take advantage of other people and they do not allow others to take advantage of them. They are more direct in communicating their needs and their preference. While they clearly communicate their wants, desires, opinions and views, people who profoundly love themselves tend to respect other people's wants, needs and opinions. They do not judge others and they do not feel that they should change or fix other people. More importantly, people who constantly practice self-love have healthy boundaries. They do not allow people to meddle with their lives and they do not meddle with other people's lives. When you accept yourself completely, you do not have the urge or need to be accepted by others. Here's how you can practice self-love:

Say positive affirmations every morning – Positive affirmations can do wonders in your life. It can fill your life with love and happiness. You can find several affirmations online or you could make your own affirmations.

Take time to meditate – Meditation shuts off negative energy and allows you to focus on the positive.

Enjoy life – If you are a codependent, you have spent so much time taking care of other people that you have already forgotten to take care of yourself. Enroll in a yoga class, dance class or travel. Go to the beach often, if that's what makes you happy. Take time to hang out with your old friends and take time to go to dinner parties.

Learn something new – Expand your skills and make yourself better. You can learn a new language or learn how to play guitar, crochet or you can go to pottery class. You can also visit the local museums and libraries. Go back to business school if that's what you want or get a master's degree. Follow the desires of your heart.

Live in gratitude – To be happy, you have to appreciate whatever it is that you have. Take time to appreciate and be grateful for your job, family and life in general. Savor that plate of baked macaroni. Stop and appreciate the view. Be grateful and you will no longer feel the need to manipulate or to let others take advantage of you just to be happy.

Always do the things and actions that honor you and respect you – Do not ever allow abusers and toxic people in your life. Do not engage with people who bring you down. Do not participate in activities that are harmful to you.

Believe in your self-worth – Understand that your worth is not dependent on someone's approval. You have to know and understand that you are worthy of love and respect. Once you realize your own self-worth, you will be surprised with how your life will change in a positive way.

Let go of the need to change and fix other people – To conquer codependency, you have to let go of your need to control other people's lives. You must let go of your need or desire to change other people. This is one of the powerful ways to heal and cure codependency. Allow people to be themselves and resist any urge to try to change them and make them better. This means that you have to stop the care taking, rescuing, controlling, apologizing and pretending. You have to also avoid making rules for other people.

Create and define your personal boundaries- This is ultimately necessary if you want to conquer and cure your codependency. Personal boundaries are basically decisions that you make about the behaviors that you will and won't tolerate.

If you have weak boundaries, you will tolerate just about anything. You allow people to hurt you and disrespect you. You also inappropriately assume responsibility for other people's mistakes, problems and experiences. If you have strong boundaries, you know where your responsibility ends and where others responsibilities begin. You draw a line between your concerns and the concerns of others. You stand up for yourself and you communicate your displeasure when someone is being hurtful or disrespectful to you.

Remember that setting boundaries is not enough. You have to enforce them. You have to communicate your feelings openly and honestly and call out people who violate them. Here are some easy steps on how you could create boundaries:

Decide what you will and will not tolerate. Take time to reflect and determine what behaviors are tolerable and what behaviors are absolutely unacceptable. Prepare a list of acceptable and unacceptable behaviors.

Watch and determine certain violations of your boundaries. Other people may not be aware that they are crossing your boundaries so it is important to communicate with others what your boundaries are. For instance, you do not want to take work related telephone calls during your day off. You must clearly communicate with your coworkers that you would appreciate it if they will not contact you on weekends about work-related matters.

Enforce your personal boundaries by calling out people who violate these boundaries. Respectfully but clearly communicate that you will not tolerate these kinds of behavior. Directly express your displeasure and then present a possible solution or alternative.

Be true to yourself – Most co-dependents have completely forgotten about their needs and desires. You have to maintain your personal integrity and be completely honest about who you are, what your dreams are, and how you feel. To heal a relationship, you have to be completely honest and become more genuine. You also have to stop caring about what other people think of you. You just have to live in the moment. Realize that it is okay not to be perfect.

Leave when you have to – Finally, when you think that you cannot change the course and the nature of your codependent relationship, it is time to leave and end the relationship. If you decide to end it, you have to end it in a healthy way. Experts say that a codependent relationship automatically ends whenever you stop responding to your partner in a codependent way. The relationship automatically ends when you set healthy boundaries and enforce it. Remember to avoid drama. Ending a codependent relationship should not be emotionally charged. Just stay calm and just communicate that if your partner could not respect your boundaries, wants and needs, then it is best to end the relationship.

Once you follow these steps, you will be surprised with the positive changes in your life. You will be happier. Your career will thrive. Your relationships will be healthier and you will be able to get rid of the diseases associated with codependency like depression, anxiety, and emotional pain. You will be able to travel more, eat in restaurants that you really like and pick out the clothes that you prefer. You will feel empowered and confident. In no time, your confidence will reach its all-time high and you can now put your painful, codependent past behind you.

Chapter 5: How Does Codependency Develop?

While no two relationships are exactly the same, neither are codependent relationships. There is a great deal of diversity and variables within relationships, and at any given time, codependency can exist or not exist. This is why experts in the field of psychology have trouble identifying what exactly a codependent relationship is. What we do know is that people with certain personality types are prone to this type of relationship and that these habits are often learned early on, usually in childhood.

While it is possible for anybody to have healthy relationships, those who grew up with parents in healthy, well-adjusted relationships tend to have a leg up against those who were raised in a household constantly engrossed in emotional turmoil and disagreement. The idea of nature versus nurture says that the personality traits of a person are variable both by the genes of the person, but also the environment they grew up in. It would be hard to ignore the fact that a child would be affected by their environment, but also by genes from their parents.

While it may seem obvious that a child from a broken home would grow up and mimic the same habits, we must also consider the role that codependency between parent and child has on future relationships. Studies show that children who are coddled by their parents and who rely on the parents for everyday tasks will be attracted to a mate who will do the same for them.

If a parent consistently takes care of a child's every need, especially when doing things the child could easily do for themselves, they lack the confidence it takes to make it out on their own. This could be anything from cooking, cleaning, doing laundry, or even having the parents deal with conflicts between friends and classmates. When a parent plays too big of a role in their child's life, they actually teach them that they don't need to try, because someone will always be there to take care of them when times get tough. Unfortunately, as these children get older and begin looking for spouses, they look for someone they can depend on. While finding a mate you can rely on is a good trait, depending on them to do the things they can do themselves is selfish, and perpetuates the codependent relationship they had with the parent.

Another offshoot of this is with very strict parenting. Having a laundry list of rules to follow during childhood teaches discipline, but there is a fine line between learning life skills and becoming a prime candidate for a codependent relationship. Often times, if the rules are not followed, the parent can become angry or disappointed, and the child learns that they are doing well by the mood of the parents. The child can feel happy when they please their parents, and all self-worth is established through these means. The child's sole source of emotional well-being comes from the parents, and not from their own self-esteem. What they learn is that doing things right or wrong, in a very black and white way, is the basis of a good relationship. As they enter find spouses, they will carry out the same relationship. They become dependent on making their spouse happy, and if they don't their self-esteem diminishes. What perpetuates it even further is if their spouse depends on them to do simple tasks for them, making the relationship highly one-sided.

Certain personality traits are often seen in codependent relationships, and if you tend to relate to these traits, it may be time to take a closer look at your relationships. While it is not your destiny to be codependent, you may be more susceptible if you are a people pleaser. This type of person avoids conflict and will do whatever is necessary to avoid it. In childhood, these kids are often the teacher's favorite, never getting in trouble, as defying the rules would cause conflict and make their parents unhappy, the stem of their self-worth.

Further down the line, this person may fall victim to an emotionally of physically abusive relationship, as the burden of sticking up for themselves and ending a relationship would impose on their abuser. They would rather stay in the relationship than going through the conflict of ending it. Their self-esteem is so dependent on the wants and needs of their abuser, that leaving would cause inner turmoil as well, which is why so many people end up staying in these types of relationships.

People who are prone to depression or anxiety are also good candidates for codependency. Although the scientific community has not officially recognized codependency disorder as an official diagnosis, links are clear between mental disorders like anxiety and depression and codependency. This is likely because all three problems are usually caused by issues with self-esteem. When self-worth is defined by how you are perceived by others, it becomes difficult to cope with someone being unhappy with you. To remedy this, people often enter into codependent relationships in order to make them happy, or defying this lowers self-esteem, leading to anxiety and depression. Either way, it can be a very tough habit to break.

Codependency is also perpetual between generations. The environment you were raised in often dictates how you will raise your own children. The habits and parenting skills you were exposed to early on stick with you, and unless a valiant effort is made to teach your children a different way of life, you will likely end up parenting your kids the same way your parents raised you. In the case of a dysfunctional, codependent upbringing, this leaves little hope that your child will have a different life.

The good news is, once the habits you have developed can be recognized as dysfunctional or co-dependent, it becomes much easier to change those habits. You cannot stop what you don't recognize as a problem. Therefore, just by reading this book and recognizing that you may have some codependent habits, you can change that in yourself so that future generations will benefit from strong, healthy relationships with friends and loved ones.

Chapter 6: Are You In A Codependent Relationship?

If you are trying to find time to be with your partner, then there is a big tendency that you might be trying too hard to be always there for your loved one. But what is wrong with waking up, brushing your teeth, eating every meal, and going to work and back home with your partner? Even if all the Disney films and love songs are trying to say that it is part of love to always want to be with a lover, it would apparently cause you a lot of problems in the long run.

Defining A Codependent Relationship

A codependent relationship can be shaped into the most romantic relationship that you can think of where it is almost impossible for you to live without each other. You may find yourself wanting to be in the same space with the man or woman of your dreams, and be with your loved one every single moment of the day.

If you tend to think that your world revolves around your partner, and you might as well die if you separate ways, then it creates a big void in your life when you face problems, or even separation. Many people find themselves being unable to recover after a divorce or breakup when they get too used to having their loved one around.

Here are the telltale signs that you are in a codependent relationship:

1. You think that your relationship is more important than anything else

You are willing to leave your career, your family, and friends just to be with your partner. If religion forbids your relationship, then the most appealing solution is to change your faith, and nothing else. Think of it as Romeo and Juliet type of relationship – when you are going against the odds, you might as well die together because well, love is all that matters.

2. You have been a little too unselfish in your relationship.

You tend to give it all to your partner, even if it is your credit card or the last dollar in your wallet, he/she can have it. It does not matter if you would be unable to visit your parents this weekend, as long as you can be the date for the movie that your partner is dying to watch. It also would not matter if you have to work on a double shift, as long as your partner would not have to worry about paying this month's rent.

3. You put in more effort than your partner.

You would mind if your partner tells you that you have to go to the grocery alone because it is baseball night with the boys. You would also find yourself in a lot of situations wherein you put in most of your money for conjugal expenses such as house and car loans, or for your wedding. You don't mind it much that your partner does not do any of the chores at home.

4. You are disconnected from other people.

Your friends may seem to be quite distant from you because you don't show up at any of the gatherings that you are invited to. If you ever show, all that you can talk about is your relationship, or you show up with your partner. Your Facebook is entirely made up of pictures featuring you and your man, and how happy you are together. That is probably the only time that your friends and family do get to hear from you.

5. You tend to always like what your partner likes.

You never really liked Mexican food, and a year ago, you hate it. But it is the only type of food your partner eats, and if he likes it, maybe you should too. You also love to buy everything for two, and you have a couple shirt (in his favorite brand, of course) for every occasion.

You also begin loving baseball and beer, and you begin having interests in absurd positions your partner begs to do in bed. You know that you do not like lovemaking that way, but if your partner likes it, then it must be good.

6. You feel responsible for how your partner behaves.

You always see the good in your partner, and if it seems that people are offended by the way he acts in public, you serve as his PR/apologist. When your partner gets in a brawl or suddenly leaves the party, you make sure that everyone knows that he is a good person deep down inside. You see to it that everyone knows that he is just having a bad day, and that he really is a sweet guy.

7. You strongly want attention and approval.

You begin making groaning sounds whenever you see your boyfriend texts someone at work, or when he is watching TV. That is your signal that you should cuddle. You also love making letters or sweet nothings more frequently now. You begin shopping for clothes that make you feel attractive. You like to shop with your boyfriend so that he can tell you the clothes that you should wear. You like yourself better when he tells you that you are beautiful. You don't feel beautiful when he is not around.

8. You hate being left alone.

You begin being jealous of his friends, and you do not want to sit alone in your couch and wait until he returns. On another note, you also would rather be alone than hang out with your friends. You feel that you are becoming afraid of his attention wandering elsewhere, and you wish that he'd always take you.

9. You ignore red flags, even the most obvious ones.

There are countless times that he lied to you, but it does not matter as long as he stays. You forgive him easily when he has some flings over the years, and it is okay that he slapped you or dragged you home when he was upset. He already said sorry, and you are sure that he meant it. Even if he said sorry for the same mistake for the nth time, you know that he still meant it.

Codependency Is A Problem

You may not realize it, but if one or both of you, exhibit these characteristics, you may soon find yourself in a painful situation. Even if you think that this is the right way to run a relationship, you may be gravely mistaken.

Codependency is considered a problem because it is an addiction, and it prevents you to exhibit actions that would be more helpful and nurturing to a relationship. One of those actions that are really important is becoming yourself. It is an addiction because it makes you behave in such a way that you restrict yourself by being obsessed on labels that could possibly not fit your relationship anyway. In the end, you may find yourself wanting your partner to behave in ways that you desire.

Isn't That Normal?

People would always have sets of expectations in a relationship, and that is normal. However, making you and your partner live according to those expectations may be too extreme. After all, you and your partner would soon change, and you may find out things about each other that you may not have expected.

Relationships that function well make allowances, but codependency does not. In a sense, it is that certain desire that makes you want your partner to always behave like a prince charming, or that certain obsession to make a bad boy material turn into a perfect gentleman, just the way you see in the movies.

However, you know that it may not happen, and it may seriously hurt your loved one to see you disappointed. You may also find yourself changing to fit instead into a certain type of person that is designed to fit your lover. In the end, you may not also do your relationship a favor when you do so.

Believe it or not, a lot of relationships fail because of these seemingly-normal things to do while people are still dating or already married. It appears that not a lot of people understand that there are certain allowances they should make in a relationship. One can blame it on the movies, but codependency can be seen as a serious attitude problem.

However, we live in a society that seriously tolerates it. There is the pressure of family standards, and we often try to figure out who among the people we date is the spouse-material, or not. We exist in a world full of labels, and in the end, we get frustrated when our expectations are not met. However, codependents go to the extreme, in the belief that anyone can turn out to be that very desirable person if they force compromise into the relationship. Sometimes though, compromises can become a little bit too extreme.

Chapter 7: When You Love Too Much, Maybe You Don't Love

Some tolerate and justify the abusive or toxic behavior of another, saying that they do it because they love them too much. What lies deep down is a codependent stance, born of deep insecurity and fear of abandonment.

Some people are willing to do anything or endure any humiliation in the name of love. They start from the premise that when one loves too much, there must be, above all, self-denial. That is, provide affection without conditions and forgive a thousand and one times if necessary. All in order not to lose or dislike the loved one.

Within that group of people are, for example, mothers who pay again and again the debts that their children contract. They know that this is not correct, but they end up justifying it in the name of love. There are also those people who embrace the same partner who mistreats them. They never leave them or leave them alone to return a short time later. They argue that when you love too much, no offense can break that bond.

The truth is that in cases like this, we are not facing a great love, but rather a dependency. This leads a person to experience a kind of affection that is overflowing and unmanageable. They feel they cannot live without the other. That is why they are willing to do anything except break that link. In these cases, you don't love yourself too much, but you lack love for yourself.

"The victim depends on the aggressor; there is emotional dependence. But it is that the aggressor also depends on the victim because he bases his self-esteem on domination."

-Ana Isabel Gutiérrez Saralegui-

Do you love too much, or do you need too much?

A codependent person, without realizing it, acts on a principle: I need you to need me. That is his way of building meaningful bonds in life. His essential attitude is to "rescue" the other, to serve as a buffer for any adverse consequences arising from the acts of that other.

This is accompanied by a perspective in which the other person does not matter. Their needs and desires should always be in the background. The only thing that matters is the needs and desires of the codependent. They are willing to sacrifice for them. They explain this unfair situation by merely saying that when you love too much, the limits on delivery disappear.

However, this situation causes them suffering and anxiety, mainly. When you love too much, likely, you will also have difficulty sleeping or experience a state of constant restlessness, eating disorders, or problems in other areas. They say that they love the other, but sooner rather than later, they turn their care and dedication into control behaviors, oriented in the background to keep that person tied.

I need you to need me

The distinctive feature of codependency is that on the one hand, there is someone who wishes to feel intensely useful or, rather, needed. This cannot be achieved with someone autonomous and mature. It requires a fragile person with many problems. Then a bond is formed when, on one end, there is someone with deficiencies and difficulties who does not want to take responsibility for himself. And on the other end, there is a codependent, who, in one way or another, assumes that responsibility belongs to him.

What emerges from this is an insane symbiosis—a type of relationship in which there is an abuse of side and side. In the end, there is a tacit agreement: the one "commits" not to solve his problems and the other to prevent him from doing so, in exchange for an unconditional "love." It is a neurotic entanglement that is challenging to recognize and analyze for those involved.

Therefore, the codependent feeds the abusive behaviors of the dependent—their excesses of consumption, anger, passivity, or whatever. Also, their excessive demands. What terrifies the codependent most is if the other stops needing him. In his imagination, if this were to happen, that person would probably depart from his side, for they would no longer need his protective mantle.

When you love yourself too much, perhaps what is in the background is a deep fear of abandonment. In this type of "love," suffering prevails, not happiness. They are common in people who have unprocessed childhood abuses. It results in such a situation when it is recognized that much of what is felt and done is not the fruit of love, but fear. Also, when those involved decide to cultivate self-esteem instead of projecting the lack in another.

Loving too much destroys us

When we talk about love, it seems that "more" is always synonymous with "better," and to believe this lie is to take a poisonous pill disguised as caramel. If we analyze the moments lived with the person we want and the moments of suffering abound, we have become victims of what they call "love."

To love is not to suffer; it is not to continually sacrifice and always bet on black. To love is not to be blind, it is not to justify the unmentionable or forgive any act for mercy. To love is not to depend; it is not to develop an umbilical cord that chains you to your partner.

Loving is not just a matter of quantity but quality. To love is not to overprotect, it is not to go back solving all the problems that the other sows nor to protect among children a child trapped in an adult body. And, of course, to love is not to end up physically or mentally torn; if our relationship impairs our emotional balance and even, perhaps, our health and physical integrity, we undoubtedly love excessively.

"That the love of a couple expects nothing in return is an invention of the submissive: if you give, you want to receive. It's healthy, reciprocal.

-Walter Riso-

The masks in the couple

It seems that a vast chasm between men and women separates the way of understanding and facing relationships.

Cultural ideals, the education received, the family environment in which you grew up, and even the biology itself are actively involved.

Children's experiences with their reference figures and especially with their parents, play a fundamental role in how they interact with others throughout their lives. Painful and challenging situations, emotional deficiencies, absence of essential figures, or lack of limits are just some of the factors that mark the way we seek and care.

On the one hand, some women tend to handle love by developing a strong dependence or obsession for the other person. The torrent of emotions is lived very intensely, expressed through the need for care and understanding towards the other, and adopting the role of "savior" on many occasions. Thus, it is quite ironic that women can respond with such compassion to others and remain with a blindfold in the face of the pain of their own lives.

«If an individual is capable of loving productively, he also loves himself; if he only knows how to love others, he doesn't know how to love at all.»

-Erick Fromm-

On the other hand, many men escape their emotions through externalizing forms, that is, obsessing with their work, using drugs, or turning their free time into hobbies that leave little time to think. They are usually emotional blocking strategies due to their inability to manage and understand them. They do not cope with discomfort or problems because they pose an unmanageable, overwhelming, shameful, or blaming burden, which is best avoided.

This type of behavior can occur in both men and women, but it is generally women who develop patterns of care and sacrifice as a way of seeking and offering affection, while men try to protect themselves and avoid pain through more external than internal objectives, more impersonal than personal.

When is it too much?

Many times we are not satisfied with a partner, but we deny reality by saying that it is only a bad time. We justify the experience thinking that this is how relationships are, passionate in the beginning, and tortuous to the end.

We forgive each other's actions by convincing ourselves that it will change. Or maybe we don't dare to break the relationship "for fear of hurting." Actually, behind all this is our fear of suffering, we are afraid of being alone or of not finding another person who can stand us.

Have you ever fallen in love, and the feeling was not reciprocal? Or maybe you had excellent, heady sex that made no sense, but the rest of the relationship was an ordeal. Perhaps you have discovered yourself acting like a mother with your partner, or you think that without a person by your side, nothing makes sense.

The situations that we have been able to live with when we interact with other people are very diverse, and therefore there are also many mistakes we make and forms of self-deception that we invent to soften the pain.

"Guilt, shame, and fear are the immediate motives of deception."

-Daniel Goleman-

Maybe if we stop to analyze how we act with someone and how our partners usually act with us, we can find pieces that resemble each other, chapters that are repeated over and over again, even if it is a different person. Partners come and go in our lives, but we stumble upon the same stones.

There comes the point where we are immersed in a vicious circle, which only repeats itself. We are unable to leave and do not even know how we got there. Again the same dramatic melody, the same bitter chords, and although the orchestra is different, the conductor is still you. Although the person is different, although the vital moment you are in is different, although you promised not to go through the same thing again, there you are again, loving too much, and also severely.

The traces of the past

Why does this happen to us? The patterns we learn at an early age to relate to others are very fixed. We have been practicing them for a lifetime, and trying to abandon or change them is threatening and a terrible challenge. But it is more challenging to realize and be aware of the reality of the situation, to be able to see from within everything that is happening.

The key is to begin to understand each other, to ask ourselves why we continuously look for someone to care for or protect, why our voice is cut off when we try to explain what we feel, and end up abandoning the task. Why do I need to know what the other person is doing and control them when they are not next to me or why, despite the suffering, do we continue to maintain a relationship that is dead?

If our way of relating hurts us and hurts the person next to us, but we do nothing to understand and change it, life will not be a way to grow but a struggle to survive.

If loving is painful, it is time to love yourself to stop the pain.
"Loving oneself is the beginning of a story of eternal love."
-Oscar Wilde-

Chapter 8: Crossing De-Nile To Recovery

Often times all the above leads to dysfunction in marriages, this becomes the cause and effect of troubled parenthood and dysfunction in Family, on a whole. The troublesome marriages end up in a divorce or separation, for which the children bears the fruits.

Parenthood as a Co-dependency Parameter

Co-dependent Parents

Co-dependency of Fear in Parenthood is one of the most general occurrences of co-dependency in parenthood.

Over consciousness: one of the effective stabilizing of a parent's co-dependency is through their acts from over-consciousness. As they are perpetually worried about their kids, they establish a argument that is paranoid, whenever the kid raises a topic.

Holding authority over all personal decisions: is one category of parents, who tend to believe that they have the right to exert authority over all of their child's decisions, regardless of their importance.

Over-bonding Parenthood: some parents try to bond too much to their kids by becoming the creepy or interfering element in their personal space, peace and calms that the kid grows up to be paranoid of everything in their life. For example, a kid hates anyone touching their stuff in a shared hotel room. This owes to the fact that her mom had a nosy habit of going through her personal belongings by utilizing the excuse of cleaning her room. One day in her hostel, the friends, unaware of this fact, try to surprise her by cleaning the room. She reacts vehemently to their surprise. This is one of the impacts of over-bonding parents who create an image of creepiness or endless interference on their account, toward the kids.

Having No respect for the Kids: another category of poorly co-dependent parenthood is reflected through having no respect for the kids. This arises from a constant judgement of the kid being irresponsible, incompetent, unable and worthless, from the parent. Hence, the parent consistently makes remarks that emphasizes their lack of respect, honor and positivity towards the kid. This recurrent disapproval from the parent can mold the kid into a terribly depressed, clueless, dishonest and useless person with perpetual failures.

Comparing the kids with others: this is one of the worst aspects of poor parenthood, where the parents keep on comparing their kid's and expectation against the peer group of neighbor's, brother's, sister's, relative's kids grades, achievements and scores.

Biased relationship with kids: sometimes parents end up treating kids separately within the family. Exemplifying, in a family of kids- 1 boy and 1 girl, mother's undue affection towards the son, can instill a sense of abandonment for the girl child while a father's attachment towards the daughter can result in the son in the family feeling detached from the dad.

Control-freaks: yes, this category of co-dependent parents also exist. Parents who exert and execute their desires upon the dreams and ambitions of the kids figure into this category of control-freaks. They specify hard and fast rules that control the academic and personal life of their kids, without any relations, breaks or rewards for the same.

Recurrent punishments: another aspect of co-dependent parenthood is where the parents involve the kids in recurrent and regular punishments for their deeds. Control-freaks type of parents establishes hard rules, for which they make strict punishments, regardless of the deed. This instils a sense of fear, hatred and discontent towards the parents.

Unsatisfied attitude: this arises from the perpetual comparisons and discontent from the parents towards their kids. Gradually the child ends up disbelieving in his or her abilities, skills, talents and dreams owing to the feeling of not making the parents ever happy. Lack of appreciation for good deeds, mature decisions and responsibilities bring about a constant depression and despair in the kid.

Perfectionists: some parents become too inflexible that they deny any fun or frolic to their kids. Their ideals of perfection remain the limits, restrictions and discontent for the kids. This inflexibility not only damages the parent-child relationship, but also brings about mentally unsatisfied kids.

Co-dependent Kids

Co-dependent kids are the kind of children who believe that their parents should be responsible for each of their deeds. Hence, they consult and counsel with their parents to achieve anything or take any a decision. This is due to their psychological belief of lacking confidence in the self about taking any decision by themselves. Co-dependent kids fear of the day that their parents will not be there, to guide them. Some of the main cause and effects of co-dependent behavior towards parents are:

1) Worried Attitude: the first and foremost cause and effect of a co-dependent child is his worried attitude. The worried behavior is consistent regarding taking any a decision, doing anything or even forming an opinion about something.

2) Perpetually Clueless: almost all co-dependent kids share this attitude as they feel clueless when they lack guidance from their parents. They do not know of an independent route or path unless guided by their parents beforehand.

3) Empathies with parents too much: co-dependent kids empathies with their parents too much that their experiences are all lived by through their parent's shoes. Empathy involves relaxing one's own desires that the subject ends up feeling more than obliged to the parents.

4) Call parents for everything: a co-dependent child ends up seeking his parents counsel under all circumstances, regardless of its importance. There is no independent identity, plan or resolutions

and hence the child lacks any motive of the own, to achieve anything.

5) Worried about crowd or loneliness: another primary defining aspect of a co-dependent child is his or her worry about facing the crowd or being lonely, in the absence of parents. Co-dependent kids cannot are highly introverted sans their parents support.

6) Love Addict: another important category of co-dependent children are the love-addicts, Casanovas or playboys. This kind of children become addicted to hunting for love due to the detachment they feel with their parents. Co-dependent children who miss their parents love, care and affection believes in being content through a relationship or constant dosage of intimacy shared with a person.

7) Having parent's dream as own dream and none of the own: often, the kids who are overly co-dependent, end up believing in their own existence as something that is heavily obliged to making their parent's dreams come true.

8) Self-sabotage: when a child ends up believing that parent's dreams, fantasies and desires are above their own, they end up sabotaging their own commitments, desires, fancies and whims to pave way for the parents dreams and ambitions coming true.

9) No self-respect: a co-dependent kid has very low self-confidence, self-esteem and self-respect that he does not believe in his own potential of realizing his dreams, as there are none. Gradually such a kid turns into a terrible automaton without no individual aim, personal success or ambition.

Family as a Co-dependency Parameter

Co-dependent parenthood and co-dependent parent-child relationship in the longer run can induce a dysfunction in the entire family. Certain times the co-dependency manhandled in a marriage are a cause of dysfunction in the family. A co-dependence scenario of troubling parenthood gives rise to co-dependent kids who pave way for a dysfunction in the family, on a full scale.

Some of the harmful effects of dysfunction in a family due to co-dependence is through

1) Lack of emotional contentment is one of the basic effects of a dysfunctional family as the kids and the parents both feel that the family is draining much of their positivity into it, rather than making themselves feel positive or content.

2) Lack of Communication instils a huge gap in the family members as in the due course of time, each family member resorts to avoiding the company of the rest for one's own peace.

3) Divorce: this is one of the direct effects of poorly handled marital co-dependencies. When co-dependency becomes irresolvable, parents can end up in suggesting divorce or separation, which can directly affect the physical, mental and emotional psyche of the kid.

4) De-valuing the suggestion of the family members: with the growing discomfort, individual members of the family ends up valuing the suggestions and remarks of

other family members on a lesser and increasingly lesser honor.

5) Lack of Love: another important effect upon a family owing to inter-dependent co-dependent parameters is the experience of immense lack of love. This instils a feeling of needing to search for love outside the family, even becoming a love addict in the process.

6) Lack of Self-respect: another quite important aspect of co-dependency in a family is the lack of self-respect among individuals as well as lack of respect for each other. This induces a feeling of constantly minimizing the value of one's family as well as dismissing the same with worthlessness. This also instils in the family, a sense of lack of aims, ambitions and achievements.

7) Lack of Freedom individually, due to controlling, hard and punishing authoritarian patriarchy by the co-dependent parents/ kids;

Chapter 9: Changing A Codependent Relationship

If you or a loved one is involved in a codependent relationship, the mental (and potentially physical) ramifications of staying in that unhealthy pattern of behavior are far too great to continue going on that way. You run the risk of developing mental and physical exhaustion, and the effects can be both short-term and long-term. Moreover, you may become neglectful in other important areas of your life, such as friendships, family, work, or health. In order to achieve a healthy relationship and an overall sense of wellness, you must be willing to adapt and foster your relationship so that it can move away from a place of codependency. The detrimental impacts of codependency can become deep-rooted issues in a person's relationship, but that doesn't always mean that splitting up or ridding that person from your life is the only solution. Yes, sometimes the best answer is getting out of the relationship, especially if there is physical harm that's been done. But if both parties are able to recognize the fact that there is an issue present, and the relationship hasn't reached the point of physical abuse or intentional emotional abuse, then there's a chance that conditions can be improved.

Oftentimes, codependency stems from a person's upbringing. As we mentioned earlier, a child who has been raised in a codependent family situation is much more likely to have the behaviors transferred to him or her. Thus, without any conscious knowledge of it, a person can be carrying around behaviors that will lead to codependency. These behaviors and psychological issues may be difficult to bring to the surface, but there are means of reversing destructive actions and patterns.

For one thing, if you or your loved one is suffering from codependency, you've already made a move in the right direction. Education is the most useful tool that you can use in combatting codependency, and by reading this book, you're arming yourself with the power to improve a relationship.

Next, you must make a very difficult decision and determine whether or not you can stay in the codependent relationship, or whether you want to in the first place. Oftentimes, people are afraid to leave codependent relationships, either because they're afraid of the loneliness that will come afterwards, or they're scared that their partner won't be able to live without them, or both. Nonetheless, these are not worthwhile reasons to stay in a relationship. This is the most crucial aspect you must realize when it comes to overcoming codependency: you are not responsible for another's happiness. That being said, you can control your own happiness. If, after doing some soul searching, you come to the conclusion that you truly want to end the relationship (or if you've known it all along but have been afraid to truly acknowledge it), then it's time to move on. We'll discuss ending codependent relationships and moving on healthfully in the next chapter.

Again, terminating the relationship does not have to be the answer. Oftentimes, a relationship becomes codependent overtime, possibly because both parties have fallen into a set of destructive behaviors. It is reversible, though, and codependency can be conquered with some hard work and dedication. If both parties choose to stay in the relationship and are willing to fix it, then it's likely that you'll both be able to make a full recovery from codependency. Keep in mind, though, that while you can control your own behavior and how much effort you'll put in to overcoming codependency, you cannot control your partner's level of commitment. Realize up front that it will be his or her duty to take responsibility as well.

If you want to improve your relationship, discuss the option of therapy with your partner. Couples' therapy can be extremely beneficial for overcoming codependency; likewise, individual therapy may also help codependents to recognize their destructive behavior patterns and provide techniques for banishing them. In individual or couples' therapy, parties may be led to examine some of the family dynamics that they were exposed to growing up. While it may be difficult to work through some latent emotions, bringing deep-rooted issues to the service will make way for reconstructing positive behaviors. This may also help both parties in the relationship learn to express a full, healthy range of emotions once again.

If your relationship has reached a level of codependency due to addiction, then treatment should become a priority. How you go about initiating treatment is up to you - sometimes, family members choose to stage an intervention. There's no easy, foolproof way to initiate this kind of conversation with an addict. Most likely, the addict already knows that he or she has an issue; unfortunately, you may feel that the addiction has reached a point at which you can no longer continue on in the relationship if the addict chooses not to seek help. Your relationship has reached a state of codependency, and without change, you won't be able to return to a healthy state.

If you or your loved one wants to overcome codependency, consider seeking other additional resources. Mental health centers and libraries may offer programs or materials to the public.

Overcoming codependency within a relationship may require a great deal of strength, commitment, growth, and patience from a person. If you're trying to change your ways to overcome codependency, you'll have to commit fully to embracing your own emotional, physical, and mental needs or desires. You may have to learn how to say "no" and stand up for yourself, and quit relying on making others happy in order to find self-worth.

One way to stay in a relationship that has become codependent is by encouraging each party to take part in his or her own activities or hobbies. In order to move away from codependence, a person must be able to regain his or her own sense of independence. Freedom is necessary in a relationship; otherwise, if a person becomes suffocated by his or her partner, feelings of resentment can build up.

The goal in overcoming codependency in a relationship is to make small changes. There's no way that you and your partner will be able to change completely within one day; yet, change is necessary. To avoid becoming overwhelmed, start with small changes that you can implement and be persistent with every day.

You must be willing to consistently ask yourself if what you're doing is for you, or whether it's for your partner. If you're moving in the right direction, you'll most likely develop a firm resolve. Keep in mind that you can be both firm and loving - it's just a matter of implementing small changes to regain your own happiness and sense of self-worth.

Also, avoid the pitfall of resorting back to old behaviors, especially if your partner encourages you to "go back to the way you were." If your partner is on board with overcoming codependency, he or she will need to be supportive so that you both can make effective changes. With enough resolution, you can overcome codependency in your relationship.

Chapter 10: How To Avoid Codependent Relationships

We should get certifiable for a minute: we overall feed off of the imperativeness and perspective of the people around us. It is uncommon that you can feel blissful in case others are constantly complaining, and it is in like manner clear that a glad social occasion of woman companions can pull you out of a channel following a horrendous day of work. In any case, what happens when you feel the need or strain to constantly guarantee that everyone around would you say you are happy?

"Human fulfilling" can to a great extent walk a practically insignificant distinction of codependency. This absurd kind of people fulfilling may incorporate lacking insistence, strain over saying "no" or sharing feelings in fear it may upset someone close to you, or even a tactless reliance on another's the response that can impact your mentality and confidence.

These attributes much of the time first structure in our gathering of the beginning stage (or as I like to suggest it, the social preliminary lab of our puberty). Focus child clung between to contending family, ring a bell? Shouldn't something be said about coping with a constantly wiped out parent or relative? Or on the other hand even a posterity of partition needing to help a doing combating gatekeeper. Now and again the lines in a relationship can get clouded, and the over-enmeshment of a social or family relationship can incite us circling our character around that relationship.

Directly, human fulfilling can appear in a sound way: unselfishness is a dazzling property! In any case, for codependents, it is less about generosity and logically about an unwanted need to guarantee people around us are managed and satisfied. Underneath everything is fear of expulsion and a yearning for outside endorsement. It's connected to requiring or on any occasion, requiring constant underwriting from others.

A large number of individuals think about "codependent" anyway less can obviously describe what codependent conduct is. Thusly, we should begin there. A codependent relationship is a spot one individual has a super energetic or mental dependence on another person. So to speak, one individual breeze up expecting an unnecessary measure of obligation for the relationship while the other individual takes essentially nothing.

The Criticalness of Points of confinement

We can best comprehend codependent connections by first contemplating how points of confinement describe sound connections. Imagine that you and your accomplice are confronting each other with a couple of feet segregating you. On the ground between you is a clearly pulled in line that loosens up to the other side and right the degree that you can see. That line portrays your "property." Everything on your side of that line has a spot with you: your contemplations, slants, body, decisions, tendencies, etc. In like way, everything on your accomplice's side has a spot with them. The idea is to accept full obligation for what is yours while being respectful of what doesn't have a spot with you. It is a ton of like being incredible neighbors.

In contrast, codependent connections are depicted by indistinct or non-existent farthest point lines. As opposed to simply expecting risk for what is yours, there is a strong inclination to step over the line and accept on included obligation for some of what has a spot with your accomplice. This is praiseworthy conduct for people who have addictive affinities and the people who will, by and large, get into a relationship with them. To put it in property owner's terms, it would look like cutting your neighbor's grass for them since they do such a poor action of it. You legitimize crossing the property line by saying it will "help" them.

For example, accept that you and your accomplice experience genuine troubles settling the conflict. When there is strain among you, he will, by and large, shut down truly and stops talking. You, understanding he isn't incredible at communicating his feelings, try to "coax him out." Nevertheless, the harder you work, the more he rebukes you with his self-important calm. Instead of resolve, your undertakings lead to growing partition in your relationship.

In this situation, your conduct reflects codependence in light of the way that you are wandering over the point of confinement line and tolerating accountability for your accomplice. It is not your commitment to coaxing feelings out of him. In a sound relationship, each individual accepts risk for sharing their contemplations and feelings paying little respect to whether they are terrible at it. Right when you more than once step over the line, you send the message that your accomplice does not need to acknowledge accountability for that bit of your relationship since you will do it for him. This set up an interminable circle that is hard to break and prompts various comparable sorts of codependent rehearses.

You Do You, Let Others Do Them

There are ways to deal with avoid getting into codependent connections or break out of codependent structures. Here are five sounds ways to deal with a start:

Settle futile not as much as respect in your connections

Make an effort, not to negligence or breaking point comments or practices that seem, by all accounts, to be belittling or impolite, paying little respect to whether it is inferred as "comical." A strong relationship is one where you regarded. If you feel attacked, put down or ousted, make some clamor and state to such an extent. In like way, you should extend a comparable worth and respect to those you care about.

Know about as far as possible line

A conventional self-keen request from time to time present: what in this relationship has a spot with me and is my commitment and what has a spot with the other person? You should endeavor to be as clear as conceivable of where that breaking point line is and stay on your side. There are specific sorts of surely understood connections that recurrent deplorable models from your past where you may feel the strong disassemble to cross the line. However, presenting yourself this request can every now and again empower you to remain grounded and keep the farthest point set up.

Make an effort not to give yourself away

Various people have fallen into codependent connections by becoming what some call "accommodating individuals." This conduct of endeavoring to be perfect in other people's eyes, by and large, has roots course again into the gathering of beginning stage. Regardless, when you give yourself away as a byproduct of being cherished or worshiped, you in like manner lose some segment of your personhood. You have to uncover to yourself that you reserve the option to be a whole individual and similarly as you are whole would you have the option to have a truly stable and satisfying relationship.

Have and worth your body

In a culture where sexual contact can seem, by all accounts, to be more like a recreational activity than an announcement of critical relationship, it becomes especially fundamental to regard your body. Your body is a bit of your farthest point obligation. If you treat your body as an expansion of your soul, you will hold that bit of you for the people who truly merit it. For example, if you would incline toward not to be contacted, state to such an extent. Your words have to control when built up in confidence. Disregarding the way this may appear common sense, various adults have unconsciously disconnected their bodies from their inward personality and end up paying a high excited cost for it.

Recognize and live inside your obstacles

Notwithstanding the way that various people live as if they have no limitations, we cannot escape from the manner in which we live with limits on all sides of our lives. Connections that are continually pushing against the point of confinement lines may look and feel invigorating from the beginning yet generally lead to inconvenience. People who push against limits ordinarily do not have the foggiest thought where the line is or even that there is a line that should be respected. Do whatever it takes not to see how close you can come to the edge before you lose your equalization. The goal is to live inside the property lines that portray you.

Reconnect with your friends and family

Right when you get too put assets into your relationship, you may out of the blue ignore other individual ties that are correspondingly critical. This is, of course, off the mark to your friends and family in light of the fact that your accomplice isn't the primary person who merits your time. You are not just someone's significant other so doesn't allow your relationship to immediate for as far back as you can recall.

More than that, the closeness of your loved ones is also a constant update that you have to regard your various commitments for the duration of regular daily existence. Also, would it say it isn't comforting to understand that you have a strong sincerely steady system outside of your relationship?

Set Boundary Points

While we are sure that your accomplice does not for the most part personality track with when you complete your own things, there may be times that, it is optimal to just offer him a little relief. There are things in life that you should make sense of how to do alone. You cannot by and large be a housekeeper in a tough situation who sits inactive yet hold on for your Mr. Impeccable to shield you from a dull task. That is not the means by which certified capacities. You have to recognize the manner in which that your accomplice will not, for the most part, be near to all day every day and that is okay. You don't have to do everything together, at any rate.

Your world doesn't have to stop when your accomplice isn't anyplace close. There are such enormous quantities of activities that you can oversee without truly needing his support. Use this opportunity to become dynamically careful and progressively independent. Everything considered it's irrefutably all the additionally compensating to fulfill a task without depending upon anyone.

Concentrate on self-improvement

Codependent connections come with colossal measures of restrictions. Your decisions for the duration of regular day to day existence, for instance, are routinely compromised in light of the way that you are compelled to compose your relationship more than everything else. Shockingly, this demeanor just keeps you from pushing ahead.

Keep in mind that it's completely fine to put yourself first. You don't have to feel remorseful about it in light of the way that there is nothing incorrectly about expecting to create yourself. It just suggests that you regard your freedom and your own dreams. Thusly, consistently keep your whole deal targets close to your heart and never lose focus.

Sentiments of contempt much of the time make when couples get so got up to speed in their connections that they disregard to consider the more noteworthy things for the duration of regular daily existence. Remember that extraordinary connections bring encouragement while the horrendous ones bring frustration. Along these lines, acknowledge the open way to look for after your individual targets while in spite of all that you can. It's never past the indicate where it is conceivable repeat yourself.

Recognize your value

We understand it's a little trendy expression anyway practicing confidence is up 'til now the best hypothesis that you can make. Right when you finally make sense of how to recognize your worth, you become aware of the things you genuinely merit. It's a sort of individual reinforcing that a considerable number of individuals need to recover themselves.

Recognizing your value gives you the courage to avoid a codependent relationship since you would now have the option to rely upon yourself to choose the correct choices. You finally comprehend that you don't for the most part need to conform to your accomplice's decisions since you're as one. You are the fundamental individual accountable for your life and your character is decidedly not portrayed by the individual you're dating. So don't consider your relationship a way to deal with complete yourself. You're perhaps deceptive yourself in case you acknowledge that true happiness can simply come from your accomplice. A portion of the time, all it really takes is just a little self-appreciation to have an imperative impact.

Instead of being a holy person, demand help

Most codependents abhor mentioning help. We would incline toward not to appear to be weak and would particularly need the unmatched activity of assistant. Regardless, it's not reasonable to do everything yourself and not require anything from others. Mentioning help is run of the mill and central and it can diminish consumption and scorn which can torment us when we have an inclination that we have to do everything ourselves.

License chance of information.

One of the essential traits of strong families and affiliations, even countries, is a chance to express contemplations and observations. Favored bits of knowledge and no-talk standards are common in pointless families. For instance, preventing the notice from securing grandma's limp or daddy's drinking trains adolescents to be terrible and to scrutinize their recognitions and themselves. Adolescents are regularly inquisitive about everything. This is strong and should be encouraged, not squelched.

Exhibit your children respect

Exhibiting gratefulness infers that you tune in and focus on them, which communicates that what their character is and what they think and feel have worth and authenticity. You don't have to concur with what they state, yet checking out comprehend exhibits that you respect them and shows them pride. Address your children with courtesy. Avoid investigation, which is harming to confidence. Or maybe, approval the conduct you need. You can set cutoff focuses and explain negative consequences of conduct you need despise without loudly manhandling or scolding, for instance, "It angers me and others when you tie up the washroom for thirty minutes. We're inside and out continued stopping," as opposed to, "You're silly and inconsiderate to tie up the bathroom. When you approach your child with concession, they will approach others with respect and foresee the identical in future connections.

Recognize your adolescents' feelings.

Various clients uncover to me that they weren't allowed to express shock, complain, feel hopeless, or even get stimulated. They made sense of how to suppress their feelings. This becomes risky in their adult connections and can provoke hopelessness. With true objectives, regularly watchmen state, "Don't feel bleak, (or burning, etc.)" or "Don't talk boisterously." Empowering youths to express their feelings gives a strong outlet. Suppositions needn't be practical, nor do you have to "fix" them. Or maybe, comfort your children and let them understand you love them, rather than endeavor to work them out of how they feel. Communicating notions doesn't infer that they should be permitted to catch up on them. Tommy can dislike his sister, yet it's not okay to hit her.

Respect your adolescents' points of confinement.

With respect to's contemplations and feelings is a strategy for in regards to limits. Clamorous assault and attacks dismiss their points of confinement, as does unwanted touch and sexual introduction or closeness. This moreover incorporates tickling past a child's comfort level. Likewise, children's property, space, and assurance should be respected. Scrutinizing their mail or diary or conversing with their companions in spite of their great confidence is inaccessible.

Grant adolescents age-fitting decisions, commitment, and opportunity

Codependents have issues choosing decisions and being interdependent seeing somebody. Adolescents need support in making sense of how to issue clarify and choose. Gatekeepers generally bungle on one remarkable or the other. Various adolescents must be understanding of adult obligations too much energy and never make sense of how to get or rely upon anyone. A couple of youths are controlled or ruined, become dependent and don't make sense of how to choose their own choices, while others are provided unfathomable open door without guidance. Converse sorts normally marry each other. They have an out-of-balance marriage, where one life accomplice manages the other, and both despise it.

Children restrict control since they search for balance. They ordinarily push for the opportunity, which isn't rebellion and should be encouraged. Age-legitimate cutoff focuses show them balance. Exactly when they're set up to test their wings, they need bearing to empower them to choose their own decisions notwithstanding the chance to commit and pick up from mistakes.

Have reasonable, obvious, compassionate guidelines and controls.

Codependents experience adolescence in homes where there are no norms or the standards is unforgiving and firm, or inconsistent and self-decisive. Adolescents need a shielded, obvious, and sensible condition. Right when standards and orders are optional, unforgiving, or inconsistent, as opposed to picking up from bungles, kids become angry and nervous and make sense of how to question their people, authority, and others. Standards should be unequivocal and consistent, and watchmen ought to be combined. Rather than base standards and trains on emotions at the time, altogether consider what's critical and what is reasonably enforceable, which changes as youths age and are dynamically independent. Unveil rules to progressively prepared adolescents, empower them to address you, and have legitimate legitimizations to back up your decisions.

Research has shown the physical order can provoke energetic issues in adulthood. The best teaches are reasonable, others conscious, and relate to the ordinary consequences of wrongdoing.

Bolster your youths

You can't give them an overabundance of worship and comprehension. This isn't destroying them. Some parent uses endowments or not setting limits to show love, anyway this is authentically not a substitute for compassion and affection, which are central for adolescents to form into confident, revering adults.

Codependent connections can be kept up a vital good way from, anyway it requires a deliberate effort to continually discover the point of confinement line and be relentless about doing exactly what is yours to do.

Chapter 11: Why Codependents Have A Hard Time With Breakups

Codependents have an exceptionally difficult time with rejection and breaking-up. It often causes irrational guilt, fear, shame, and anger. It can also trigger hidden grief.

Codependents often blame their partner or themselves.

Codependents will often have loss and trauma from childhood triggered with a breakup.

Codependents see their relationship as being the most important to them.

Codependents fear that this could be their last relationship.

Codependents have low self-esteem, so when they are rejected, it triggers shame.

Codependents often haven't grieved their childhood.

Let's look at some important issues that if you work through them, can help you to let go and be able to move on.

Blame

Poor boundaries are one of the main signs of codependency. You might have trouble seeing others as unique individuals, with needs, motivations, and feelings that are independent of yours. You might feel guilty or responsible for the actions and feelings of others. You might even project blame if you feel ashamed or guilty. This can make you highly reactive, and it can cause you conflict in your codependent relationship.

In fact, one person's need for space or even the desire to breakup isn't necessarily the result of his/her partner's behavior. Just because you blame your partner doesn't make it their fault. There are sometimes instances where your abuse, infidelity, or addictions, precipitate a breakup. Those are behaviors based on individual motivations and they are part of a much bigger picture of why your relationship fell apart. You are not responsible for the actions of someone else. People have a choice and they chose what they are going to do.

If you are angry or resentful it can keep you stuck, not able to move out of the past. Codependents often blame others, because they have difficulty being accountable for their own behavior. This includes not setting boundaries or asking for their needs to be met. As a child, they may have been blamed. Over time this has become a learned defense to shame that protects them from a sense of guilt that is overdeveloped.

Low Self-Esteem and Shame

Shame from a young age within a dysfunctional family can lead to codependency. Codependents believe that they are flawed, and that in some respect even unlovable. Children see themselves as being rejected and shamed by the parental behavior, even when it's not meant to be. Even if your parents professed their love, they may have still behaved in a manner that you understood to mean you were not loved for the unique person you are. Communication is not always clear, and sometimes things are said that a child takes out of context.

The shame we experience is sometimes at an unconscious level, and it can drive you to love someone who can't love. In doing this, the fact that you believe you are unlovable is self-fulfilling without your conscious even being aware you did it.

Sometimes a codependent will shame themselves by making negative comments about themselves. For example, 'I'm a failure or I'm defective.' You might run those types of scripts through your head blaming yourself for all that goes wrong.

When you have low self esteem, it can lead to a cognitive self-evaluation, which in turn leads to you putting fault on you because of the defects you feel you have. You might also find yourself using this form of thinking when a relationship ends that you did not initiate. Suddenly you blame yourself for everything that went wrong in the relationship. It is important for you not to do this.

Maggie's Story

Maggie's partner cheated on her, not once but a number of times. Maggie, because she is codependent and has low self esteem, assumed this happened because she was not attractive enough, no longer desirable, and that it was all her fault. None of this was true and Maggie's believe came from her fear of intimacy. Once Maggie learned to love herself, her shame was healed and her self-esteem grew.

The Last Hope

The loss of a partner can be devastating, and even more because you are a codependents, so you put very high value on creating a relationship that makes your partner happy, and ultimately you interpret the breakup as a failure on your part.

Fear grows out of shame. When you are ashamed, it translates to a fear that you will not be loved or accepted. As a codependent, one of your biggest fears is being alone, being abandoned, because you think you are not worthy of love. It's common for a codependent to cling to an abusive relationship where they are always emotionally abandoned. The problem is as a codependent the fears you have aren't rational. Build a life that you enjoy, a life that you can live single or with a partner in a healthier relationship where your happiness isn't all dependent on your partner.

Grieve Your Past

Codependents have difficulty letting go, because they have trouble letting go of their childhood hope that they will receive the kind of love they want from their parents. They expect their partner to love them, care for them, and accept them unconditionally in the manner they had wanted their parents to. The problem is a partner simply cannot make up for those losses and early disappointments in your childhood. Parents are far from perfect, and even those that are good parents, will disappoint their children at some point. One of the big steps in becoming an independent adult is to realize and accept this, emotionally and intellectually. That means you need to grieve, which makes you sad and can sometimes make you angry.

Past Trauma

Psychologists will tell you that each new loss recapitulates an old loss. You may have already had losses in your adult life that compound the grief of what you are going through now. Many times, it is your abandonment loses from when you were a child that is the trigger.

As a codependent you may have been blamed, neglected, abused, rejected, or betrayed in your childhood, and current events cause these traumas to be reactivated. Sometimes, they unconsciously provoke situations reminiscent of your past to heal you.

You might also perceive rejection when it's not there, that's the way you expect to be treated. Part of grieving is learning to let go, but in the process it is very important to make sure you keep friendships that are important and life affirming activities. Guilt, shame and blame help you in no way, but if you take the time to work through your past traumas you can go through your feelings and figure out exactly how you feel at the end of your current relationship. You might be surprised at what your true feelings are after you work through your past traumas. You might not actually miss them, but rather you miss what they stood for in your relationship.

Whatever you are feeling it is important to acknowledge to so, then accept, and let go. To heal you must accept yourself and your partner as two separate entities. Generally, a relationship ends, because your partner has issues related to self-esteem, shame, or they are not a good match so they can't communicate openly to fill each other's needs.

Shame tends to cause people to withdraw or turn away from the other important person(s) in their life, especially a partner. You need to heal your trauma and deal with your loss(es), which in this case is your breakup, then start to build your self-esteem so you can move forward with your life and you'll be responsible for you. You won't rely on anyone else. This approach will change any future relationships, you might have.

Relationships are the Answer

When you grow up in a family that is dysfunctional and insecure, you develop your own strategies and defense mechanisms so that you can feel loved and safe. Some codependents will withdraw completely, others will seek power, and still others will attempt to win their parent's love by adapting to the needs their parents have.

A typical codependent will continue to try to make relationships work, often much harder than their partner, in order to feel okay with themselves. They solve their insecurities and inner emptiness through a close relationship. Once a codependent is in a relationship, it's pretty common for them to drop their hobbies and interests including their friends. All of their energy is focused on their relationship, the partner, the one they, which actually not only damages the relationship, it damages them.

Some couples spend their time talking about their relationship, rather than actually enjoying their time together. When the relationship ends, they experience a deep emptiness without their partner. Remember, your happiness begins within you. To begin to recover from a codependent relationship you need to take responsibility for your own happiness.

You may no longer really have a 'life' outside of the one with your partner. It's important to find things that make you happy, reconnect with friends or make new ones, and look for 'joy' wherever you go.

You might need the help of a 12-step program – that's okay!

It's important to have things that bring you happiness and pleasure, whether you are in a relationship or single.

Chapter 12: Codependent Relationships

Relationships are precious and complicated, with many conflicting, illogical and wonderful aspects. No relationship is perfect, and sometimes it might be difficult to see that the common issues of partnerships have become more unwieldy and difficult than normal.

There are many indicators that can suggest whether you are in fact experiencing a codependent relationship. In the general sense, it is usual for one partner to enable the other by supporting their vices, whether they are irresponsibility, immaturity, addiction or even poor health. By supporting this enfeebled partner it allows their behaviors to be validated and continue without improvement. This ultimately is not healthy and cannot be sustained, causing massive strain on the relationships.

That is not to say that these relationships are loveless failures. A key and important part of codependent relationships is that they form close bonds. Bonds borne out of the intimacy and love necessitated in the support offered and received, respectively. Indeed such struggles against adversity often reinforce a deep emotional connection through the shared experience.

We can see each of the six patterns clearly at work here. The helper feels a sense of responsibility for their partner, possibly believing that their partner could not survive without them. The helper will also likely feel guilt at the thought of leaving their partner to struggle alone, preventing them from abandoning the relationship for their own sake. This is a heavy motivator for the helper to try desperately to change their partner's life for what they may correctly, or incorrectly, believe is for the best. Also, in comparison to their dependent partner, some sufferers may feel a false sense of superiority, and a bolstering of self-esteem in the wake of their perceived belief of the incompetency of their partner. In any case this balance requires an abnormal amount of control or compliance on behalf of one or both partners.

Whilst this dynamic could be seen to be a loving and dedicated partnership, especially by those in the relationship, in reality it is simply how each person has learned to gain affection. This involves refusing to look at their personal self-esteem and control issues and is ultimately self-destructive.

It is important, therefore, to have a close look at your own relationship to make sure that there are no such unaddressed issues. Below are some common signs that are generally considered to be indicators of a codependent relationship.

Partners often struggle to make any decisions regarding their relationship. Those who look to their partners for strength and stability find themselves unable to make decisions on their own terms. Due to the inadequacy they feel for themselves, which is reinforced either intentionally or innocently by the care giver, they believe that they are incapable of making correct decisions. This is governed by a deep fear of losing their partner and support. The care giver conversely, cannot make decisions due to the overwhelming guilt and loyalty to their partner, hindering their judgment and forcing the care giver to abandon their own desires.

This fear and guilt will inevitably make it difficult to analyze their own feelings. Both partners will define their own feelings in the context of the other person and their relationship. Their own low self-esteem will bolster their reliance on each other, and will enforce a stronger bond of attachment which may be perceived as true affection rather than the emotional crutch that it has become. This untangling of your true feelings for the person, from those of obligation and ego fulfillment, becomes increasingly difficult.

With all these considerations, it is likely that communication in the relationship has become strained. By hiding their true feelings from themselves it will make it impossible for the partners to convey their feelings to each other. Also by being unable to make decisions regarding the future of the relationship, it is likely that many and even well meaning discussions will descend into arguments. This is due to the fact that nothing new will ever be brought to the discussion and nothing will be resolved, resorting to repetitive and therefore irritating discussions.

The constant reliance on your partner, either for support or for self-assurance boosted by a false sense of superiority, will cause partners to lose trust in themselves. For those being enabled by their partner, the reliance on the care giver will lead to the belief that they are hopeless. The care giver, however, will find that a less indentured society will not provide them with the adoring audience that they are used to, and they will find their ego severely wounded.

Needless to say all of the above will reinforce a severe fear of abandonment in the partners. This will often manifest itself in the constant craving for approval and validation from their partner. The reinforcement by their partner will satisfy this craving, resulting in a vicious cycle which is difficult to break from.

This will eventually result in your mood being totally dependent on your partners. Your own self worth will hinge directly on their treatment of you. However, even if you begin to feel that your partner no longer respects you and treats you in an acceptable manner, you will still crave approval from them. This often leads to simmering resentment of your partner but an inability to leave them due to the fear of abandonment and the feeling that your self-worth is contingent on their approval.

This will often lead to guilt, shame and embarrassment. If you choose to share the situation with friends or family they will often be confused as to why you choose to stay in the relationship. This often only serves to embarrass suffers further, as they find it difficult to convey the complex psychological issues involved. Indeed sufferers may not even understand why this is happening, leading to further charges of inadequacy against themselves.

If you feel that you or your partner, even a member of your own family, or a friend is experiencing any of these patterns, then they may be suffering from codependency. It is a debilitating, complex and often undiagnosed disorder. It takes great courage to admit that what you are feeling is perhaps beyond the normal realm of emotion. However, now that you have taken that amazing first step, the rest of this guide will show you that recovery is not only possible, but something well within your own grasp.

Chapter 13: The Habits Of Codependent Individuals

Please people at their own expense
Codependents are people-pleasers, that is, they try their best to satisfy the needs and wants of everybody around them. They are always the first to respond to calls for help. The "hero" chromosome in them always pushes them to the front queue of helpers and saviors whenever one is needed. They have an intense need to provide help, and they feed it upon the problems of their friends and family members. Often though, they provide help and care at their own expense. They go the extra lengths even if it means getting burned to make themselves indispensable to anybody that might require help

Discomfort with receiving attention or help from others
Unfortunately, codependents do have scruples with asking for and receiving help. They have been conditioned to keep their

emotions and needs close to their chest while growing up and cannot bring themselves to show what they see as weakness. Therefore, they suffer in silence. They don't ask for help and would rather brave the waters on their own. When they receive help such as cash gifts or an unsought for recommendation, they get discomfited and confused about how to react. Therefore, they keep themselves in positions where people don't even know they require help. They may even cover up their lack with an apparent projection of having in excess. Even from the same partner they are codependent upon, they find it hard to take anything apart from appreciation and more requests for help.

See themselves from the eyes of other people

Codependents are some of the most self-critical individuals on earth. Their lack of self-esteem means they are forever insecure and wary of other people's opinions and perception of them. As such, they may out up a fake lifestyle to impress people while remaining essentially hollow inwards. They do not react to negative criticism well and may either respond aggressively or go out of their way to avoid criticism entirely. Most importantly to them though, they are obsessed with how their partner views them. Does he see them as totally indispensable? Are they the only port of call when he runs into trouble again? These are the most important questions that run through the minds of codependents.

Conveniently ignore red flags

Especially in their relationships, codependent individuals always seem not to see the obvious signs. Largely inspired by their dependence on their partners and a reluctance to rock the boat or avoid conflict, they avoid fixing problems within their relationships until it is too late. They keep glossing over warning signs and refuse to heed warnings and obvious hints.

Rationalize the mistakes of others

This is the crux of codependency after all. They are always there with a readymade excuse as to why their partner isn't up to social standards. Alcoholism? Well, he had a troubled childhood. Gambling addiction? He doesn't really gamble that much. Besides, he is rich. Their library of excuses never gets exhausted. Even when the partner obviously recognizes that he has a problem that needs to be solved, they would rather remind him they are there rather than join hands to find a lasting solution.

Give more than they receive in relationships

It is constant in codependent relationships that one party gives out more care, attention and affection than the other. Individuals suffering from codependency constantly subdue the voice of their own needs, do not demand for much if anything at all and are too afraid to speak out their minds. Therefore, it is not surprising to see them constantly giving out more than they receive. Anyways, most of the time, their partners may have "bigger problems" that cries out for their attention than taking stock of the attention they receive.

Have loosely defined boundaries

Boundaries are important in every relationship. They are necessary to ensure that you don't get trampled upon. There has to be limits beyond which you won't go or tolerate. Your friends, family members and partners have to pay you some respect and not overstep their bounds. A boundary helps you mark a fine line to divide your finances, feelings, emotions and needs from that of your partner. Unfortunately, codependent relationships have undefined, poorly defined or blurred boundaries. Partners see themselves as an extension of the other half. There are no limits and invariably, emotions and desires get trampled upon. Codependents do not set boundaries because they want to remain open and be the first port of call for as many people as people when crises arise.

Say yes all the time

A codependent does not know or use the word "NO" to any request. He never opts out of giving a service if he can, no matter the lengths he has to go to provide it. This doesn't mean that he is totally comfortable with all tasks though. He has just been configured to make himself inconvenient before he thinks of disappointing any other person. Against the backdrop of a childhood most likely spent seeking the good graces and approval of difficult parents and probably unyielding siblings, it is easy to understand why the thoughts of turning down a request might be so foreign to a codependent individual.

Feelings of guilt or responsibility for the suffering of others

The initial phase of codependency stems from a heightened sense of responsibility and duty to help other people overcome their sufferings. Especially for people who became codependent as a result of having to cater to the needs of an ill friend or relation, they become filled with the idea that they are the only ones in a unique position to help every other person around them. Therefore, they feel heavy guilt when they are unable to stem the tide of suffering that an associate is experiencing. They see it as a failure when they are not considered to help alleviate suffering or when their ministrations fail to yield positive results. They therefore relax their boundaries and limits lower to further cater for others. Their show of care is the only thing that gives them joy and satisfaction and when people suffer, it raises a sense of guilt in them.

Reluctance to share true thoughts or feelings for fear of displeasing others

Children who grow up to be codependent are taught not to show emotions or admit weaknesses. They grow into adults incapable of intimacy. Intimacy in this instance does not refer to sexual activity although it has also been found to be affected. Intimacy in this context refers to the ability to share their feelings, emotions and desires with their partners and be capable of demanding for their rights as equal partners. Scared of displeasing people or thinking they may offend people by asking for help, they keep their true feelings within them and play to the gallery.

Chapter 14: Road To Recovery

Many of the common traits of codependency is something that we have all experienced to lesser or greater degrees. Many of the issues are simply part of what makes us human. Indeed codependent relationships seem to contain greater and stronger bonds than perhaps some typical relationships, by helping each other in times of adversity.

So some of us may ask, is being codependent actually that bad? Well not always. Isn't it good to want to help others out? Isn't a respect for not always letting our emotions run unguarded a good thing?

There will always be aspects of the 'patterns' in all of us. However, the old motto of 'everything in moderation' seems particularly apt here. It is when these behaviors, even the seemingly good, altruistic ones, become suddenly exaggerated. Altruism, while good in small doses, can become a two edge sword when it leads us to deny our own happiness, or leads others to become dependent on you, forsaking their autonomy.

So, recovery is certainly desirable, but is it possible?

Like all things in life it requires work and perseverance but yes, recovery in even the most serious cases is more than possible. By looking at the symptoms and acknowledging that you can see those traits in yourself is the first difficult step. Engaging with the disease directly and not avoiding it is a momentous step towards recovery.

Is recovery possible?

Codependency is a disorder that is deeply rooted in our everyday behaviors, thoughts and feelings. With other addictions sufferers have the options of completely cutting out the object of their addiction. Alcoholics can choose, with willpower, not to drink again. Codependents however, cannot just physically separate themselves from their own feelings.

Recovery therefore involves a great deal of discipline and self help. Sufferers must put a great deal of personal effort into their recovery. Learning to become independent of the crutches built around them is a difficult but an incredibly freeing process. By letting go of the vast amount of energy it takes to care for another, or manipulate those around us, it can enable us to focus productively on more fruitful pursuits.

Recovery from codependency means focusing on you and excluding all the bonds that you have built around yourself. It involves taking on responsibility for your own feelings, actions and behaviors. You must learn to accept yourself and love yourself for who you are, without being defined by those around you.

The standard treatments are self-help, group therapy and individual sessions. You have taken the first step, that of self-help, by purchasing this book. Hopefully you will be able to bring around the changes in your life by helping yourself. Nevertheless, you should always know that other options are available to you, even if you never need to use them.

With all these tools many people have successfully recovered from their codependent habits.

Chapter 15: How Did You Get Into A Codependent Relationship Anyway?

If you followed the advice in the last chapter, you should have resolved most if not all of the character flaws that may have gotten you into a codependent relationship in the first place. Nonetheless, it is still good to address this topic so that you can use the information for future relationships.

As we've already mentioned and will see in more detail in the next chapter, manipulative people tend to prey on those with low self-esteem issues. They know that if you do not have confidence in yourself, and that it will be easier for them to take advantage of you. It is not your fault that there are predatory people like this out there just as it is not your fault that car thieves exist in the world. However, if you want to protect your car, or in this instance, yourself, it is good to know the types of things that attract a coercive person to their prey.

Lack of family members or support is another characteristic that will draw a predator toward you. Whether it is a family member themselves, a roommate or a significant other, the pattern is the same. The person will usually guilt-trip you from spending time with others in order to alienate you from the other relationships in your life.

As mentioned before, and contrary to what popular media tells us, men tend to be the predominant manipulators in our society, whether it be in personal relationships or situations at large. The reasons are twofold. One, because they usually are in higher positions of authority, and so are in a better place to prey on those with vulnerabilities. And two, because men are predominantly raised in ways that nurture a sense of entitlement in them toward things that they do not have a right to. Men are taught to take when women are taught to give. If this idea seems ridiculous to you, think about how many times the women in your life, or yourself, if you are a woman, are in situations where they are serving food, doing the laundry or any other household chore (giving) while men in your life, or yourself, if you are a man, are sitting around playing a game or watching TV (taking). Even when both partners in a heterosexual relationship are working, women tend to do a predominant amount of the housework. This is all to say that if you are a woman, that is another target on your back from manipulative predators.

While there is nothing you can do, or should have to do, about being a woman, you should simply be aware of how some men operate. When you are interacting with a man, especially in the earlier stages of forming a relationship, notice whether he tends to speak with you or at you and look out for a tendency to keep unreasonably asking or expecting things of you. While not all manipulative men pounce right away, if they are exhibiting those traits, these could be warning signs to watch out for something worse down the line.

Though it has already been mentioned several times in this book, it cannot be stressed enough that another person's harmful actions toward you are never your fault. This chapter is only meant to make you aware of the possible characteristics that manipulative people seek out when preying on others. By having this information handy, you are better informed and in a better position to fend off any unwanted and harmful relationships.

Chapter 16: Free Yourself From Codependency And Take Control Of Your Life

If you or a loved one is involved in a codependent relationship, the mental (and potentially physical) ramifications of staying in that unhealthy pattern of behavior are far too great to continue going on that way. You run the risk of developing mental and physical exhaustion, and the effects can be both short-term and long-term. Moreover, you may become neglectful in other important areas of your life, such as friendships, family, work, or health. To achieve a healthy relationship and an overall sense of wellness, you must be willing to adapt and foster your relationship so that it can move away from a place of codependency. The detrimental impacts of codependency can become deep-rooted issues in a person's relationship, but that doesn't always mean that splitting up or ridding that person from your life is the only solution. Yes, sometimes the best answer is getting out of the relationship, especially if there is physical harm that's been done. But if both parties can recognize the fact that there is an issue present, and the relationship hasn't reached the point of physical abuse or intentional emotional abuse, then there's a chance that conditions can be improved. Thus, without any conscious knowledge of it, a person can be carrying around behaviors that will lead to codependency. These behaviors and psychological issues may be difficult to bring to the surface, but there are means of reversing destructive actions and patterns.

For one thing, if you or your loved one is suffering from codependency, you've already made a move in the right direction. Education is the most useful tool that you can use in combatting codependency, and by reading this book, you're arming yourself with the power to improve a relationship. Next, you must make a very difficult decision and determine whether or not you can stay in the codependent relationship, or whether you want to in the first place. Often, people are afraid to leave codependent relationships, either because they're afraid of the loneliness that will come afterward, or they're scared that their partner won't be able to live without them, or both.

Nonetheless, these are not worthwhile reasons to stay in a relationship. This is the most crucial aspect you must realize when it comes to overcoming codependency: you are not responsible for another's happiness. That being said, you can control your happiness. If, after doing some soul searching, you conclude that you truly want to end the relationship (or if you've known it all along but have been afraid to acknowledge it truly), then it's time to move on.

Again, terminating the relationship does not have to be the answer. Often, a relationship becomes codependent over time, possibly because both parties have fallen into a set of destructive behaviors. It is reversible, though, and codependency can be conquered with some hard work and dedication. If both parties choose to stay in the relationship and are willing to fix it, then it's likely that you'll both be able to make a full recovery from codependency. Keep in mind, though, that while you can control your behavior and how much effort you'll put into overcoming codependency, you cannot control your partner's level of commitment. Realize upfront that it will be his or her duty to take responsibility as well. If you want to improve your relationship, discuss the option of therapy with your partner. Couples' therapy can be extremely beneficial for overcoming codependency; likewise, individual therapy may also help codependents to recognize their destructive behavior patterns and provide techniques for banishing them. In individual or couples' therapy, parties may be led to examine some of the family dynamics that they were exposed to growing up. While it may be difficult to work through some latent emotions, bringing deep-rooted issues to the service will make way for reconstructing positive behaviors. This may also help both parties in the relationship learn to express a full, healthy range of emotions once again. If your relationship has reached a level of codependency due to addiction, then treatment should become a priority. How you go about initiating treatment is up to you - sometimes, family members choose to stage an intervention. There's no easy, foolproof way to initiate this kind of conversation with an addict. Most likely, the addict already knows that he or she has an issue; unfortunately, you may feel that the addiction has reached a point at which you can no longer continue in the relationship if the addict chooses not to seek help. Your relationship has reached a state of codependency, and without change, you won't be able to return to a healthy state. If you or your loved one wants to overcome codependency, consider seeking other additional resources. Mental health centers and libraries may offer programs or materials to the public. Overcoming codependency within a relationship may require a great deal of strength, commitment, growth, and patience from a person. If you're trying to change your ways to overcome codependency, you'll have to commit fully to embracing your own emotional, physical, and mental needs or desires. You may have to learn how to say "no" and stand up for yourself and quit relying on making others happy to find self-worth. One way to stay in a relationship that has become codependent is by encouraging each party to take part in his or her activities or hobbies. To move away from codependence, a person must be able to regain his or her sense of independence. Freedom is necessary for a relationship; otherwise, if a person becomes suffocated by his or her partner, feelings of resentment can build up. The goal of overcoming codependency in a relationship is to make small changes. There's no way that you and your partner will be able to change completely within one day; yet, change is necessary. To avoid becoming overwhelmed, start with small changes that you can implement and be persistent with every day. You must be willing to consistently ask yourself if what you're doing is for you, or whether it's for your partner. If you're moving in the right direction, you'll most likely develop a firm resolve. Keep in mind that you can be both firm and loving - it's just a matter of implementing small changes to regain your happiness and sense of self-worth. Also, avoid the pitfall of resorting back to old behaviors, especially if your partner encourages you to "go back to the way you were." If your partner is on board with overcoming codependency, he or she will need to be supportive so that you both can make effective changes. With enough resolution, you can overcome codependency in your relationship.

Being Aware of Codependent Thoughts and Behaviors The fact that you are still reading shows that you are a courageous person. You are ready to at least think about how codependence could be affecting your life. Take a moment to feel good about your bravery. Now comes a hard part of the process of overcoming codependence: recognizing your codependent behaviors. To begin, start a journal where you can keep track of your thoughts and actions. Do not judge your reactions. Merely state what they are, close your journal and get back to living your life.

Here are some things to watch for and write down.

• When your partner makes a mistake, what do you do about it?

• What do you think and do when your partner criticizes you?

• How do you feel when your partner disagrees with you?

• Do you ever spend money on or go out to buy things for your partner that you know he shouldn't have?

• Which of your thoughts and behaviors are aimed at controlling your partner's problems?

• What do you do to help your partner keep his job?

- What do you think about when your partner hurts you either emotionally or physically?
- What do you think and how do you feel when your partner blames you for something?
- How do you feel, and what do you think about when your partner is upset or angry about something that happened to him away from home?
- If there are children in your household, what do you think and do when your partner complains about their behavior?
- What do you do to keep the peace in your household?
- What do you think and do when someone requests of you, and you are unsure about whether you can help them? Do you say yes, even if you don't feel up to the task?
- What do you think and do when you don't live up to your expectations?

These are only a few things you might notice as you go through the next week. Be honest as you write in your journal. It is for you and you only. Study yourself carefully. Remind yourself that facing reality is hard, but that once you do it, you can move on to getting healthier and happier. Where Are Your Boundaries? A major part of codependence has weak or inappropriate personal boundaries. Get your journal and something to write with for the next exercise. Mark on your page the numbers 1 to 10. Now, read the following statements and rate them anywhere from 0 and 10. 0 means you do not agree at all, five means you neither agree nor disagree, and ten means you completely agree.

Here are the statements to rate.

- What is mine, and what are my partners.
- I am not responsible for my partner's behavior.
- I am a worthwhile person with or without my partner.
- I have my purpose in life, aside from caring for my partner.
- I care about my partner's feelings, but I do not take them on as my own.

- I allow others to have their own space. I don't move so close to people that they back away from me.
- I am content with myself and with life in general regardless of the opinions of others.
- I agree to help others who ask for help when I can, but I say no when I do not feel comfortable helping or when the request is beyond my abilities.
- It is more important to care for myself than to please other people.
- Other people, including my partner, can have their own opinions without hurting my feelings. I don't feel the need to have other people tell me I am right.

Were you honest with yourself? If so, add up the numbers to rate your acceptance of personal boundaries. The lowest possible score, of course, is zero. The highest possible score is 100. Where does your number fall? The higher your number, the healthier your sense of appropriate personal boundaries is. If your number is lower, especially if it is below 50, you have problems separating your own identity from the identities of others. This is an indication that you can benefit from working to overcome codependent thoughts and behaviors. How Do You Feel About You? Codependent people usually have very low self-esteem. Codependent people often feel inadequate in their abilities.

It is only by managing their partner's addictions that they can experience a sense of self-worth. If your partner was no longer a part of your life, who would you be, and what would you think of yourself? Here are a few questions to think about as you consider your independent sense of self-worth. Write your answers in your journal.

• Do you make decisions based on your own set of values?

• Do you need others to tell you that you are attractive?

• Are you capable of making your dreams come true?

• Who decides whether you are a good or bad person?

- How can you tell if you are intelligent or not?
- Whose needs come first – your needs or the needs of those around you?
- How do you feel when you fall short of perfection?
- How do you react when someone compliments you?
- Do you like to keep your own company?
- Do you get uncomfortable when others approach you to socialize?
- Do you isolate yourself to keep from getting hurt?
- Can you put aside any guilt feelings that come up when your partner has problems due to his addictions?
- Do you like who you are?

If these questions are hard to answer or make you think about yourself in ways that you would rather not consider, you are not alone. People who struggle with codependency tend to feel threatened when they constructively examine their thoughts and actions. It is much easier for people who are codependent with a partner to blame themselves or others than to own their feelings, thoughts, and behaviors, and let others own theirs. Loving you and putting your feelings first can be a radical departure from the way you have been thinking of yourself and others. It is a hard process to go through, but it is the first step to breaking free of codependency.

Evaluate Your Evidence After a week is up, find a quiet place to be alone and sit down with your journal. If your partner does not like to give you privacy in your home, stop by a park, and sit on a bench. Read through your journal and think about whether or not your thoughts, feelings, and actions during the week fit the profile of codependency.

Notice the times you put others (especially your partner) ahead of yourself. Look for ways you took responsibility for your partner's addiction issues. Did you say anything positive about yourself? Or did you criticize yourself for the decisions you made? If you are not sure whether or not you are displaying signs of codependency, read through the book this book again until you get back to this section. Then, look over your journal and honestly assess your level of codependence. Once you see the pattern, it is time to learn about enabling and how you can avoid it.

Chapter 17: How To Fix Codependent Relationships

A codependent affair may be extraordinarily deplorable, for the codependent individual and rest around that individual. The individual on whom you are codependent probably will not have a ton to recognize subsequent to the nonattendance of care or desire to not comprehend is particular of the grant components of codependency. A codependent individual will begin disregarding their prosperity, will set wrong needs for the duration of regular day to day existence and would relentlessly make rancor everlastingly and for everything around that individual.

The best technique to correct codependent ties initiates with recognizing codependency

1. You ought to recognize codependency and recognize that you are codependent. This is tough just as someone is dependent

on a different person, either truly or rationally, fiscally or in a greater number of ways than one. But in the event that an individual recognizes that the individual being referred to is codependent, one won't have the will or the arrangement to fix the issue.

2. At the point when codependency is recognized, a line or a couple of lines

be going to be strained. All codependent conduct must stop. In this case, if a life partner has an alcoholic spouse, then the wife should not like the husband paying little heed to how crushed he is. This may be burdensome to do anyway it must be effected. A line must be drawn. If a man has a narcissist sister, by then he ought to stop driving the narcissistic conduct. As opposed to pushing or subbing for the narcissist sister's conduct, the kin should empower her to recognize the cold hard truth of the world. In a wide scope of codependency, the codependent individual accomplishes various objects, which are not to the best bit of leeway of the relationship and without a doubt not strong to the codependent person. Each should not engage codependency by footing the offender, dependent individual or one with a character issue. As opposed to engaging, every single encouraging movement or feedback should be ended instantly.

3. A result must be chosen. That may not be careful toward the began anyway by and significantly a month or months one must have the choice to see the completion of the entry. Do you intend to linger in the relationship? Do you the inclination to leave the relationship and establish another life? Do you wish to recover the relationship absolutely? The reaction to these requests would choose how uncommon or how evaluated a procedure you should have.

4. Searching for master aids is significant for all things considered. Codependent people are likely not going to be adequately ready to catch up alone. Months or significant lots of codependency make by far remarkably powerless-willed and besides engrave the

confidence. Searching for or having capable aids will implement a codependent individual to have an aching and the self-restraint to see by way of catastrophes

5. More huge than anything, one needs to fix the purpose behind codependency. The secret of how to mend a codependent rapport distorting in the patching of the issue which could be substance abuse, mental issues or character issue. The occasion the essential driver is disposed of, never again insist codependency continue nor would the glue be a codependent relationship. Revamping the rule issue is significantly more troublesome than one may anticipate. It requires some investment for people to discard alcoholism or a long time and a huge amount of attempt and master aid to fix character or mental issues. Regardless, this is likewise the terrific means to deal with amend a codependent relationship. There is simply unusually a great deal of an individual can supposedly and request to manage to locate the issues of

codependency if the fundamental concern actuating codependency still continues on.

6. It may not by and large work yet conversing with the individual with whom one offers a codependent relationship may be a shrewd concept. In case the other individual is adjusted or efficient and if the relationship is commonly fulfilling in various habits, then discussing and having a collective procedure can be very helpful. A concerted means is compelling since both the people in the relationship would then have the option to make some little walks, in their own specific habits conferring to their scope and quality, to patch the issue. Right when two people cooperate, it has a huge mental influence, which is altogether constructive. Conversing with an alcoholic life partner, sitting and watching out for the issues, persuading someone to forgo substance exploit or if an individual recognizes their blunder of physically misusing the other individual and after that stops it, by then how to mend a codependent relationship turns into a cakewalk.

7. Fixing a codependent relationship necessitates a long trip. It is a long walk around the circumstance. Additionally, that walk is not basic. Having belief is indispensable and one should in like manner be completely conscious of the conclusion that is charming. There is nothing incorrectly in removing a codependent relationship, as it is definitely common to endeavor to patch it. It is imperative to have a conventional genuinely strong system as watchmen, companions, family relatives or someone who can give the quality and continue rousing one to continue further, conquer every trouble.

Concentrate Independently Confidence

Concentrate on the way in which you converse with yourself. Replace negative self-thoughts like, "I am terrible enough," with positive ones like, "I am meriting worship correspondingly as I am." Focus on your characteristics as opposed to your constraints. Endeavor to consider frustrations to be open entryways for improvement, and for the love of llamas quit scolding yourself for what your accomplice does!! You are not their gatekeeper.

If you find that it is a model for you to draw in with people with addictions, it is okay to examine whether you might be a "fixer," yet do it with confidence. Endeavor to be intrigued, rather than judgmental about your models. Almost certainly, this is something that started in your immaturity (as portrayed above) and it is not your lack. I understand it will, in general, be disturbing to look at your own special models, yet it is very much defended, regardless of all the issues. In case you have to start that journey, it is verifiably something that we can manage in treatment.

Something that I like to do with my clients is to empower them to make sense of how to "re-parent" themselves. Basically, you make sense of how to relate to yourself as if you were the careful, worshiping gatekeeper that you never had. It might sound nutty, yet it really works.

How Might I Quit Being Codependent In A Relationship?

Enable Consequences To happen

If your accomplice will be late for work since he's been pulled over for a DUI, don't delude the boss for him. Give the trademark consequences of his moves an opportunity to take place. Once in a while, the primary way an addict can give indications of progress is by hitting "outright base," and that can't happen if someone is continually covering for them.

Sometimes, it will feel exceptional to permit these to consequences happen. For example, if you have to kick your companion out of the house, you may feel like an appalling person. You aren't! I've even known mothers who have expected to hang on and watch while their adolescents go to detain. This isn't straightforward, yet the alternative is to continue to impede the activities that the dependent individual direly needs to make sense of how to feel pushed to change.

Guidelines to Stop Being A Codependent Engaging operator: Know Your Cutoff points

Comprehend that "NO." is a complete sentence. Recognize what your cutoff focuses are and stick to them. One way to deal with do this is to channel your body for your own one of kind notions. Acknowledge when something makes you uncomfortable and give yourself the approval to put a stop to it, paying little respect to whether it might make your accomplice upset. Make sense of how to offer need to your own special slants of comfort, instead of constantly endeavoring to fulfill your accomplice.

Characterizing sound points of confinement is one technique for truly loving yourself. Commonly people who will when all is said in done ignore cutoff points are pulled in to the people who haven't the foggiest how to set them. Do whatever it takes not to envision that your accomplice should know when your get is being pushed. You should be anxious to express "NO," and would not kid about this.

Stop Being Codependent: Focus On Yourself

This is a significant one. Become increasingly familiar with yourself better. Discover what you like and what you don't and figure out how to fill your reality with a more prominent measure of what you like. Make courses of action with companions and don't hold up until you understand your accomplice is difficult to reach to make plans! Guarantee that you are practicing self-care (eating extraordinary, working out, getting enough rest, etc.) and empower time to discover relaxation exercises that you welcome that do exclude your accomplice. It's useful to have interests outside of your nostalgic relationship. A couple of individuals stress this could obliterate their connections, yet the converse is truly clear. Having individual interests makes each person in the relationship sit back and relax pondering themselves, and this makes a progressively favorable couple.

Furthermore, when you have your very own jam, you have more stimulating things to examine when you do contribute vitality with your accomplice.

Connect

Above all, understand that there is help open! Try examining one of Melody Beattie's works like her significant book, "Codependent No More," which has helped millions. Or on the other hand, discover an Al-Anon meeting, which is a sister meeting of Alcoholics Puzzling, for accomplices and loved ones of those suffering from addictions.

Understanding that you aren't in this situation alone is an incredibly astonishing resource. It can help you with feeling less isolated, and it might even empower you to recognize other individuals who accomplish fundamentally the same as things that you do. This will empower you to become conscious of why you think and feel that way that you do. It's very retouching to recognize why you act the way wherein that you do; this is what we call "becoming conscious," and it's the pathway to enthusiastic chance.

Look to Your Past

The underlying advance on your approach to security is to research your own one of a kind past to uncover and comprehend encounters that may have contributed to your codependency. What is your family heritage? Is there eager negligence and abuse? Were there events that provoked you isolating yourself from your genuine internal emotions and ignoring your very own needs?

This can be a problematic strategy and one that incorporates contemplating and re-encountering youth sentiments. You may even find that you feel angry, awful, terrible or accountable as you consider this.

Note: This sort of examination can be amazingly energetic and upsetting and is normally best done in a secured treatment relationship.

Recognize Renouncing

The second way to repairing is to genuinely be straightforward with yourself and recognize the issue. There doubtlessly a phenomenal plausibility you have intellectualized and upheld your codependence after some time. While it can feel alarming to confess to being codependent and furthermore connected with a messed up relationship, dependability with yourself is very the underlying push toward patching.

Disengage and Disentangle Yourself

In order to truly wear down and create ourselves, we have to at first disconnect from the things we are messed with. Personal development will require giving up our interruption and over-consideration with endeavoring to control, rescue, or change others and our defaulting to continually endeavoring to fulfill someone else.

This infers taking a full breath, surrendering and recognizing we can't fix gives that is not so much our own to fix. What issues do we "have" and what issues are "asserted" by others in our lives? It's about genuinely endeavoring to isolate where you end and others start.

Practice Self-care

Giving up your undertakings to constantly fulfill others is a better than average beginning to recovering, anyway learning self-care is completely significant too. It's unreasonably critical that you really begin to explore and become aware of your own insights, feeling, and needs. We in like manner need to make sense of how to communicate them to others in our connections. This may feel hard and even new to us from the beginning as if you are all around especially narcissistic. Notwithstanding, that is a bit of making sense of how to manage our very own needs.

Self-care means managing ourselves physically — eating healthy, getting enough rest, rehearsing ordinarily, and taking off to our PCP and taking any recommended drugs. Self-care in like manner means contemplating ourselves deep down, making social connections, discovering happy positive activities to fill our time, and allowing ourselves energetic get-away and lay in case we need it. It is like manner suggests really connecting and taking a gander at our very own considerations, sentiments, characteristics, needs, and needs — paying little regard to what other's conclusions are. Extraordinary systems to do this can be composing and reflecting through the method of journaling, examining appropriate books on self-care, and of course, going to treatment.

To make a strong whole deal relationship with others, you ought to at first create a strong one with yourself.

Make sense of how to Express No!

Presumably, the best ways you can begin to characterize sound limits is to make sense of how to object to conditions that are hurting to your own one of a kind thriving. This will feel uncomfortable from the beginning, yet the more you do it, the less complex it will become. We save the benefit to oppose others and normally we don't need to give them a long explanation. We hold the choice to object to things that are not the best for us. This isn't connected to being intolerant and barbarous towards others — yet it's connected as far as possible and putting our own one of a kind needs first.

Be Self-caring First

Be minding to yourself! This is about self-compassion and treating yourself a comparable way you would treat the others you appreciate!

Here is a nice little exercise to endeavor to do this:

Close your eyes and picture your nearest companion.

By and by imagine they come to you and say they are genuinely hurting in light of the fact that something has really gone sideways in their life. They've lost a work or a relationship is struggling or they've "failed" by one way or another or another.

Would you say to them, "Well, it's feasible your blemish since you didn't do either" or "You should have contributed more vitality" or express "This is in light of the fact that you aren't sufficient or insightful enough"

Of course, you wouldn't express that to a companion. So for what reason would you say that kind of stuff to yourself?

Everything considered you would get a handle on your companion and express, "That is ghastly. I'm lamented, by what method may I help"

You ought to be big-hearted to yourself consequently, also. Treat yourself as you would treat a companion who is persevering. Make sense of how to challenge any negative, essential self-talk, and any negative convictions about yourself and your confidence.

Learn Independence

Finally, have a go at secluding from others for explicit time periods to make a sound sentiment of self-rule. Decrease dependence through making sense of how to be removed from every other person and truly making sense of how to like it! People who are codependent consistently believe that it is hard to contribute vitality alone without others around them.

Find an individual redirection or interest just for you. Go read in a coffee shop without any other person, go the movies alone, go to the activity focus alone. Discover a couple of various approaches to make an opportunity and make sense of how to contribute vitality with yourself!

Codependency can be changed and patched! Does changing this bit of yourself make you feel uncomfortable? Possibly searching for the course of a counselor might be useful as you work your way through examining how codependency impacts your life. A better than average expert will have the alternative to empower you to explore your past, your uncomfortable feelings, and encounters, and help you adjust dynamically solid strategies for relating to yourself and to other individuals.

In case you are concerned that you or a companion or relative is codependent and are enthusiastic about examining treatment, you should contact a professional asap for intervention.

Conclusion

Yes! We all have to show care and concern for the people around us; family members, friends, neighbors, associates, spouses etc. They are important components of our existence and their welfare should be our concern. But, that's where the buck should stop. Their welfare is not meant to be our life. Caring for them should not extend to become a total dominance of your affairs. Caring for them should not be the only reason why you exist. Unconditionally taking on all their problems would automatically deprive you of the space to deal with yours. In time, it will take total control of your life and make you addicted to caring for them. Your whole existence would revolve around seeking approval from them and needing to feel depended upon by them. Nobody deserves that. Sacrificing yourself on the altar of care and martyrdom as codependency preaches is not likely to help them get better. If anything, it may encourage them to remain steadfast in their troubles. Therefore, you need to learn to put your interests forward. You need to consider yourself first before you decide if you are going to be able to help. You need to be able to say "NO". "Yes men" always remain "Yes men" for the rest of their lives. They do not achieve because they have hitched the wagon of their achievement to another's rail. Given the fact that they are providing care because the other person's path does not look smooth, it should be no surprise that they often find their own progress curtailed too. One of my most favorite quotes of all time by Beverly Engel says;

Subduing your needs and desires in a relationship to take care of your partner's every whim and vagaries is not heroism; it is emotional suicide. Letting your partner know that despite his excesses, you will always be there, is no sacrifice; it is plain stupidity. Your "hero" chromosome was designed to be used as a protective mechanism for those around you, do no turn it into a double-edged weapon that cuts you and every other person within your sphere in the long term.

Always remember, you are responsible for you. You are not suffering from a lack of esteem because people trample upon your rights and desires; it is you who have opened the gates of your boundaries for everybody to trample upon. You are not codependent because your partner needs attention; you are, because you want him to need your attention. You do not feed off the dependence of your family members and friends because they need somebody to depend on; it is because you want them to depend on you. The problem is not with the people who depend on you. The problem is with **YOU**. This is the right time to get out of the whirlpool of codependency; do not dither, become free!!! Get out **NOW!!!**

www.ingramcontent.com/pod-product-compliance
Lightning Source LLC
Chambersburg PA
CBHW071827080526
44589CB00012B/944